IMPULSE CONTROL

Activities & Worksheets for Middle School Students

More than 130 Activities & Reproducible Worksheets to Help Children Learn How to "Be the Boss" Over Their Impulses

Tonia Caselman, Ph.D.
Joshua Cantwell, M.S.W.

(Grades 6 – 8)

Layout and design by Tonya Daugherty

Edited by Susan Bowman

ISBN—978-1-59850-058-5

Library of Congress Control Number:
2008909435

10 9 8 7 6 5 4
Printed in the United States

PO Box 115 • Chapin, SC 29036

(800) 209-9774 • (803) 345-1070 • Fax (803) 345-0888

yl@youthlightbooks.com • www.youthlight.com

Dedication

Thanks to my husband, Steve Jones, who has provided me with huge amounts of encouragement and task support at home. Also, thanks to all of the children who have allowed me to "test drive" many of the activities and worksheets included in this book.

— *Tonia Caselman*

Special thanks to all of the wonderful women in my life: Amy, Debra, Ashley, Norma, Maudi, Patricia, Nancy, Jamie, Judy and Betty, for giving me the opportunity to act on my impulse to love.

— *Joshua Cantwell*

About The Author

TONIA CASELMAN

Tonia Caselman, Ph.D., L.C.S.W., is an Associate Professor in the School of Social Work at the University of Oklahoma – Tulsa. In addition to teaching and research, she maintains a private practice specializing in children and adolescents. She provides supervision and training for individuals and programs. She is the author of numerous articles in addition to the books, *Impulse Control: Activities & Worksheets for Elementary School Students, All about Boundaries,* and *Teaching Children Empathy, the Social Emotion*. She is also co-author of the therapeutic games, *Boundaries Baseball, Remote Control Impulse Control* and *The Impulse Control Game.*

About The Author

JOSHUA CANTWELL

Joshua Cantwell, M.S.W., is Program Director of ROCMND-Tulsa Area Prevention Resource Center in Tulsa, Oklahoma. He is the co-author of two therapeutic games, *Boundaries Baseball* and *Impulse Control Remote Control* and has worked with children and youth in group shelter settings, outpatient treatment, mentoring and school based programs.

TABLE OF CONTENTS

PURPOSE

"I count him braver who overcomes his desires than him who conquers his enemies, for the hardest victory is the victory over self."

—Aristotle

Success in the classroom requires more than intelligence and memory. It requires motivation, organization, and impulse control. Impulse control helps students inhibit dominant responses in favor of a more functional subdominant response. The ability to decline urges to skip homework or talk to a classmate during instruction is absolutely needed to be a successful learner.

Social success also requires impulse control. Young people who interrupt, stand too close, take too much control, etc. are not well-liked by peers. Using good problem-solving skills and using good social judgment requires the ability to slow down and think.

Impulse Control for Middle School Students is designed to provide school social workers, psychologists, counselors and teachers with activities to help students think about and practice strategies to become more reflective (vs. impulsive). Using cognitive-behavioral theory and techniques, it is intended to provide school personnel with tools to teach students how to slow down and think before acting. The games, role-plays and work sheets described in *Impulse Control for Middle School Students* are presented in a playful, but thoughtful manner so that students can become easily engaged in the process of learning about and practicing impulse control. The activities and discussions are designed to:

- Teach students the value of impulse control
- Teach students how to anticipate consequences
- Teach students how to be more reflective learners
- Teach students how to manage their feelings
- Teach students good problem-solving strategies

RATIONALE

Young people who are impulsive frequently do the first things that pop into their heads without thinking of the consequences. They can interrupt or intrude on others; they can make off-topic remarks in conversations; they can overreact to minor injustices; they can rush through assignments, making multiple errors. These tendencies to act without adequate thought or planning often lead to academic and social problems.

Research shows that impulsive young people do not examine their work before beginning and are inattentive to instruction. Consequently they make poorer grades than more reflective students (Gargallo, 1993). Impulsive students are less accurate in word recognition, make more errors, and are generally poorer readers than more reflective students (Harris, et al, 2005; Nietfeld & Bosma, 2003; Roberts, 1979). Impulsive children also have more problems in math.(Cathcart & Liedtke,1969) In a more recent study, Nietfeld and Bosma (2003) found that an impulsive cognitive style tended to generalize across academic tasks (i.e. verbal, mathematical and spatial). This certainly puts impulsive children at greater risk for poorer academic achievement.

Impulsive young people also have difficulty controlling their actions which leads to problem interactions. They tend to overlook important information that would assist them in getting into "sync" with others. Indeed, close social connections require that one is able to understand and respond appropriately to another (MacDonald, 1996). Research shows that impulsive individuals have poor social problem-solving skills (McMurran, Blair, & Egan, 2002) and have problems in social relationships (Landau & Moore, 1991; Patterson & Newman, 1993). In addition, impulsivity has been associated with delinquency and aggression (Dougherty, et. al., 2007; Feindler, Marriott, & Iwata, 1984; White et. al., 1994), and lower levels of empathy and remorse (Kochanska & Aksan, 2006; Miller, 1988).

However, studies suggest that skill building in impulse control can make a difference (Baer & Nietzel, 1991; Gargallo, 1993; Teeter, Rumsey, Natoli, Naylor, & Smith, 2000). Early studies showed that modeling is useful in modifying impulsivity. Students showed more reflective behaviors after observing reflective adults (Denney, 1972; Yando & Kagan, 1968). Later studies used modeling and self-instructional training to improve impulse control (Kendall & Finch, 1978; Kendall & Wilcox, 1980). Gargallo (1993) saw significant improvement using a training program for impulsive eighth graders that included modeling, reinforcement, forced delay, the use of scanning strategies, internal speech, and problem-solving. Other studies found improved impulse control by teaching social problem solving skills (Elias, Gara, Schuyler, Branden-Muller & Sayette, 1991; Elias & Weissberg, 1990).

How To Use This Book

Impulse Control for Middle School Students is designed for small groups but can also be adapted for larger classrooms or in one-on-one counseling sessions. Each lesson is set up so that it covers a specific aspect of impulse control. All of the discussions and activities in a single lesson focus on that unique content. Lessons may be used as single session if only selected activities and worksheets are used. Or, lessons may be broken down into two or three lessons if all of the activities and worksheets are used. Sections in each lesson include the object of the lesson, a rationale for the lesson, a list of needed supplies, a suggested way to introduce the topic, discussion questions, activities, and reproducible worksheets.

Lesson 1	**Impulsivity: What the Heck Is It and How in the World Do I Control It?**
Lesson 2	**Schoolwork: Slow and Steady Wins this Race – Really!**
Lesson 3	**Problem-Solving: Problem? What problem?**
Lesson 4	**Decision-Making: Decisions, Decisions, Decisions**
Lesson 5	**Mood Management: Master of My Emotional Universe**
Lesson 6	**Anxiety: Don't Be a Worry Wart**
Lesson 7	**Anger: Is Temper-Taming Anything Like Lion-Taming?**
Lesson 8	**Empathy: How Can I Walk in Someone Else's Shoes Without Getting Athlete's Foot?**
Lesson 9	**Social Skills: Keeping It Friendly**
Lesson 10	**Boundaries: Living and Coloring Within the Lines**
Lesson 11	**Peer Pressure: Staying Strong When Others Try to PEERsuade Me**
Lesson 12	**Boyfriends and Girlfriends: Is It Really Romance or Is It Drama and Chaos?**

CREATING A CARING GROUP. Young people respond and learn better when they feel safe and cared for. Facilitators should make sure that the emotional "climate" of the group is warm and accepting. Facilitators should establish positive relationships with all of the students and make sure that students are respectful, supportive and encouraging to one another. In order to establish this, "ground rules" should be decided among the group members at the beginning of the first group. A few basic rules such as "no put-downs" and "everyone listens when someone is speaking" may be helpful in creating a safe and trusting group.

MODELING. Facilitators should absolutely model good impulse control themselves. Social learning theory suggests that as students observe us, they will imitate our behavior. Facilitators can draw better attention to their impulse control by talking about it as it happens. For example, when faced with a decision, a facilitator should say aloud "Hmmm, I need to think about this" or, when faced with their own impulses, might report, "You know, I had the impulse to interrupt you just now but I stopped myself and thought that would be rude and so I waited until you were finished talking."

VERBALIZED SELF-TALK. Young people with poor impulse control have poor internalized speech. Facilitators should verbalize their own self-talk (as in the example above) and then coach students to do the same. If a student becomes angry s/he can be coached to talk to her/himself with statements such as, "It's going to be OK. It's no big deal." If a student describes a problem, s/he can be coached to generate several solutions. If a student is beginning a task s/he can be coached to say things like, "What is my goal here?" or "What am I trying to accomplish here?" etc. If a student is working on a difficult project, s/he can be coached to say, "I need to be careful," or "I need to pay attention here," etc. Students may also need to use encouraging self-talk such as "I'm doing OK here," or "Just a little more and I'm finished," etc. Have students do this aloud and then, over several weeks, have them whisper it. As they become more skilled at self-talk they can simply think it.

PROBLEM-SOLVING. Impulsive young people are poor problem-solvers because they do not slow down enough to generate multiple solutions in order to identify the best one. Although there is a specific lesson plan in this book dedicated to the topic of problem-solving, this skill is so important in the development of impulse control that it should be used at each session. Whenever a problem or a need for a decision arises in the group, the facilitator should stop the group and ask for 3-5 suggestions on how to solve the problem.

REINFORCEMENT. Catch students using their impulse control and praise or reward them for it (reinforcement). Even the most impulsive young person is not impulsive 100% of the time. Notice when students refrain from talking or manage their anger. Praise them in front of the group or give tokens or points that can be used for prizes. Behavior theory suggests that rewards increase the behaviors that are being rewarded.

Impulsivity: What the heck Is It and how in the world do I Control It?

Lesson 1

Objective:

At the end of this lesson students will be able to

- Define and describe an impulse, and identify the steps of impulse control
- Identify personal impulse control challenges and successes
- Recognize the problems associated with poor impulse control
- Recognize the benefits of using impulse control

Materials Needed:

Dry erase board/chalkboard, dry erase markers/chalk, paper, pens (or pencils), small pieces of candy, and several games of checkers.

Script:

An impulse is the feeling, urge or temptation to do or say something. All of us have impulses. There is no shame in this. It's human. Impulses often come quickly before we have time to consider them. We might have impulses to show our anger; we might have impulses to avoid responsibilities; we might have impulses to talk at inappropriate times; we might have impulses to interrupt or intrude.

What is important, though, is asking yourself, "Am *I* in charge of my impulses or are my *impulses* in charge of me?" Being in charge of your impulses means that you know how to *stop* and *think* when an impulse hits you. It means being in charge of your life. Wouldn't it be great to be the boss of your impulses instead of having them be the boss of you?

Rationale:

There are actually many benefits of having good impulse control. Research tells us that people who have better impulse control do better in school (Nietfeld and Bosma, 2003), have more friends and get along better with their friends (Landau & Moore, 1991; McMurran, Blair, & Egan, 2002; Patterson & Newman, 1993), and are better able to handle stress (Mulsow, 2001).

Some young people may not have heard the terms impulse or impulse control. While some students will be more familiar with the term "self-control," this book will focus on the phrase "impulse control" in order to better identify what aspects of the self is being controlled (i.e. urges, feelings, temptations, etc.). As in many school lessons, it is important to introduce relevant language at the beginning of a unit so that everyone has a common understanding during discussions.

In addition, it is important to introduce the skill steps of impulse control (stop and think) in the first lesson so that they can be applied to each subsequent learning unit. And, finally, this lesson will examine the benefits and consequences of using/not using impulse control in order to enhance motivation to learn all that is available in the following chapters.

Discussion Questions:

- What are some examples of impulses from your own life? (i.e. what impulses or urges do you have in the classroom? At home? With friends?)
- Have you ever gotten into trouble for acting on your impulses? What were the consequences?
- What do you think other young people think of those who don't use impulse control? Who do use impulse control?
- How do you stop yourself when you know that you have an impulse that might get you into trouble?

ACTIVITIES:

Explain to students that in 1984 there was a movie released titled Impulse and that the tagline for the movie was "Imagine what would happen if every desire, every urge, every passion, locked deep inside all of us ...suddenly exploded." Ask students to discuss what they imagine this movie was like and what the world would be like if this were true.

Write the following quotation from Aristotle on a dry erase board or chalkboard, *"I count him braver who overcomes his desires than him who conquers his enemies, for the hardest victory is the victory over self."* Discuss students' perceptions and opinions of this line.

Give each student a pencil/pen and a piece of paper and direct them to interview an adult regarding impulsivity and impulse control. Ask them to obtain the following information: (1) what is an impulse that the adult has had in the recent past; (2) was s/he successful in controlling it or did it control her/him; (3) what were the person's feelings following the encounter with an impulse; (4) what were the benefits or consequences? Ask students to report their findings to the group.

Set one piece of candy in front of each student. Tell them that they can either eat one piece of candy now or, if they can wait five (5) minutes, then they can have three (3) pieces of candy. Wait 5 (five) minutes and reward those who have waited to eat with an additional 2 (two) pieces of candy. Ask students to identify the strategies that they used to delay gratification by resisting the impulse to eat the first piece of candy (i.e. looking away, reminding themselves of the reward, thinking about something else, etc.). Suggest to students that they can use similar strategies when they face other situations when they need to delay gratification.

Set up games of checkers for students (one game for every two students). Direct them to play according to the rules but to "talk out loud" as they consider each move. For example, a student might say, "If I move here, you might jump me so I think I will leave this piece here." Discuss how *stopping* and *thinking* helps to make better decisions.

ACTIVITIES:

Explain to students that you will be reading several scenarios where students had various kinds of impulses. At the end of each scenario ask students to describe the consequence(s) and the benefit(s) of either following the impulse or saying "No" to the impulse.

- Maria is the goalie for her soccer team. At the last minute of the game she missed a ball and the other team scored and won the game. Maria felt angry and embarrassed. She had the impulse to kick the goal post. What would be the consequences of giving in to this impulse? What would be the benefits of *not* giving in to this impulse?
- Jeremy needed to ask his mother if he could go to a friend's house but she was on the telephone. He had the impulse to interrupt her. What would be the consequences of giving in to this impulse? What would be the benefits of *not* giving in to this impulse?
- It is February and Marco is tired of the school grind. His best friend, Carlos, is going to skip class in the afternoon and walk down to a store. Marco has the impulse to join him. What would be the consequences of giving in to this impulse? What would be the benefits of *not* giving in to this impulse?
- Uniqua's math teacher doesn't seem to like Uniqua. In fact, Uniqua feels like this teacher picks on her all the time. One day in class the math teacher blamed Uniqua for talking when she really wasn't. Uniqua had the impulse to yell at her teacher. What would be the consequences of giving in to this impulse? What would be the benefits of *not* giving in to this impulse?
- Matt just started skateboarding. One night when he had a lot of English and History homework to do, a bunch of his friends were meeting with a guy who was teaching them some trick skating maneuvers. Matt had the impulse to skip his homework and go skateboarding. What would be the consequences of giving in to this impulse? What would be the benefits of *not* giving in to this impulse?

How To Use Reproducible Sheets:

Reproducible Worksheet 1.1

Impulses in Context, asks students to identify specific impulses that they struggle with in the classroom, at home, and in the community. Self-awareness can decrease impulsivity by making students aware of triggers or weak spots.

Talk about it. Ask students how easy or difficult it was to identify impulses that they struggle with. Ask students to share some of the impulses that they identified. Point out similarities between students in order to create a sense of support within the group.

Reproducible Worksheet 1.2

In the Doghouse with Impulses, asks students to think about different ways they have had trouble for acting on impulses. Prior to this exercise students may not have connected negative consequences with their acts of impulsivity and, therefore, may not have seen impulsivity as problematic. Recognizing a problem is the first step in changing the problem.

Talk about it. Ask students if they can think of additional ways that they have had trouble with impulses that they acted on. Discuss how this exercise may have motivated them to work on the problem.

Reproducible Worksheet 1.3

Think about the Consequences, asks students to match impulses on one side of the page with potential consequences on the other side of the page. Taking time to consider potential consequences for certain actions can assist students in behaving less impulsively.

Talk about it. Ask students if they can think of additional consequences for any of the impulses that were described. Discuss how frequently students take time to consider consequences before acting on an impulse. Discuss any obstacles that keep students from taking time to consider consequences.

Reproducible Worksheet 1.4

Benefits of Impulse Control Scramble, helps students continue identifying ways in which impulse control can improve the quality of their lives. Students are asked to unscramble each word and to read the phrase that describes a benefit of having impulse control. The five benefits that are listed are as follows: (1) Stay out of trouble, (2) Make more friends, (3) Feel good about yourself, (4) Make good choices and (5) Get better grades.

Talk about it. Ask students if they can think of additional benefits for practicing impulse control. Discuss which benefits are more motivating and less motivating for students.

Reproducible Worksheet 1.5

Rating My Impulse Control, uses a Likert scale to examine students' performance on specific behaviors that require impulse control (i.e. waiting, asking before borrowing, controlling temper, listening, making good choices, etc.). This is an excellent tool for self-evaluation and for helping students identify specific behaviors that are in need of further work.

Talk about it. Ask students if they completed this page impulsively or if they took time to stop and think about each response. Ask students to share those areas where they are both strong and weak regarding impulse control. Discuss ideas for how to improve weak areas.

Reproducible Worksheet 1.6

Impulse Control Remote Control, asks students to *stop* and *think* about various impulses. They are asked to decide if you should PAUSE to take in more information, REWIND to think about and learn from situations from the past, or FAST FORWARD to think about potential consequences.

Talk about it. Discuss the three (3) strategies of taking in more information, thinking about what has been learned from the past and thinking about potential consequences. Ask students to identify which of these strategies they use the most frequently and which one they need the most work on.

Impulses In Context

Look at the pictures below and write down as many impulses as you can think of in the classroom, at home and in the community.

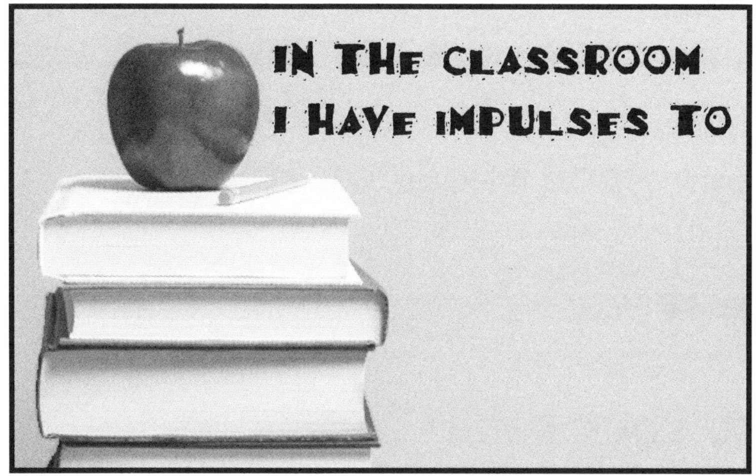

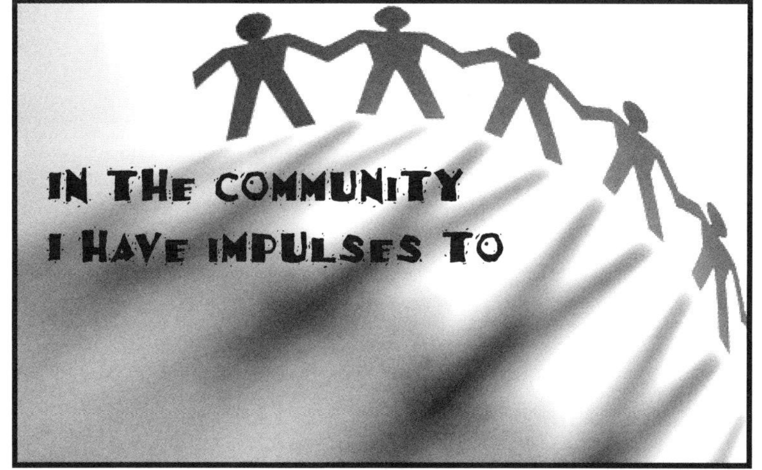

'In the Doghouse' with Impulses

Have you ever had trouble for following your impulses without stopping and thinking first?

Check the ways that you have had trouble:

- Grounded from doing things .... ❑
- Grounded from phone or computer.... ❑
- Yelled at.. ❑
- Sent to your room.............................. ❑
- Had a grade lowered .... ❑
- Sent to the principal's office .... ❑
- Had people angry with you .... ❑
- Lost friends .... ❑
- Got in-house suspension at school .... ❑
- Got suspended or expelled .... ❑

About The Consequences

Read the descriptions of impulses in the boxes on the left. Consider what might happen if a person does not *think* about the consequences. Then read the consequences described in the boxes on the right. Match the possible consequences on the right with the actions on the left by drawing a line to connect them.

Impulse	Consequence
Kenyatta told Yolanda that she had a crush on Daniel. Yolanda has the impulse to tell another friend who also likes Daniel.	S/he could get caught and be given an 'F' for cheating. S/he would also feel very embarrassed.
Oscar sees the answers to the history test laying on his teacher's desk when she is out of the room. He has the impulse to look at it and copy down some of the answers.	S/he might embarrass the other person and hurt the other person's feelings. Other kids might see her/him as a bully.
Sara is spending the night with Leela. In the middle of the night Leela suggests that they sneak some of her parents' alcohol and drink it. Sara has the impulse do it.	S/he might be wrong. Kids might get angry with her/him for being rude and making accusations without proof.
Jeremy just had one of his games stolen. He sees another kid playing the exact same game. He has the impulse to accuse him of stealing his game.	Other kids might think that s/he is a poor sport or make fun of her/his outburst.
Anna struck out in the softball game and is feeling embarrassed and frustrated. She has the impulse to throw the bat down.	S/he would be creating a conflict between two friends who she enjoys being with at the same time.
Bernardo sees Ricky's new haircut which he thinks looks silly. He has the impulse to laugh at him.	S/he could get caught and get in trouble from two sets of parents. She could also be forbidden to hang out with her friend any more.

Benefits of Impulse Control Scramble

Did you know that impulse control can really make our lives better? Unscramble the following phrases to find out the benefits of impulse control:

(1) YTAS TOU FO BETUORL.

___ ___ ___ ___

___ ___ ___   ___ ___

___ ___ ___ ___ ___ ___ ___.

(2) TGE AOGLN THWI STHEOR

___ ___ ___   ___ ___ ___ ___ ___

___ ___ ___ ___

___ ___ ___ ___ ___ ___.

(3) LFEE GDOO BAOTU SYEOLUFR.

___ ___ ___ ___   ___ ___ ___ ___

___ ___ ___ ___ ___

___ ___ ___ ___ ___ ___ ___ ___.

(4) AEMK DOGO ECIIONSSD.

___ ___ ___ ___   ___ ___ ___ ___

___ ___ ___ ___ ___ ___ ___ ___ ___.

(5) OD ELWL NI OSHOLC.

___ ___   ___ ___ ___ ___   ___ ___

___ ___ ___ ___ ___ ___

RATING MY IMPULSE CONTROL

Listed below is a list of behaviors that reflect good impulse control. Read each item and rate yourself by circling one of the numbers next to it.

1 = Poor **2** = Not so Good **3** = Fair **4** = Good **5** = Excellent

1. I wait patiently for my turn at games, at the water fountain and during other activities.	1	2	3	4	5
2. I think before I speak.	1	2	3	4	5
3. I think of several solutions to a problem before I choose one to act on.	1	2	3	4	5
4. I ask to borrow things before I take them.	1	2	3	4	5
5. I control my temper when angry.	1	2	3	4	5
6. I stop myself from laughing at inappropriate times.	1	2	3	4	5
7. I weigh out all the pros and cons before I make decisions.	1	2	3	4	5
8. I listen to others without interrupting.	1	2	3	4	5
9. I take the time to read others' feelings.	1	2	3	4	5
10. I make good choices when I am with friends.	1	2	3	4	5

Now go back and put a star by the item that you are best at and circle the one that you most need to work on.

Impulse Control Remote Control

Read the following situations and decide if you should **PAUSE** to take in more information, **REWIND** to think about and learn from situations from the past, or **FAST FORWARD** to think about potential consequences. Circle the appropriate symbol for each situation.

1. You can't find your tennis shoes and have the impulse to yell at your mom.

2. You are bored and have the impulse to bug your sister.

3. You keep forgetting to take your homework to school. You are excited to get to school to see your friends and have the impulse to run out the door.

4. You tend to get in trouble for talking in class. You have the impulse to tell your friend something really important.

5. You are at your parents' friends' house for the first time. There are other kids there your age but you don't know any of them. You have the impulse to jump in and start talking about your newest video game.

6. You are in a really cool store that has all kinds of cool electronics. You have the impulse to stick an ipod in your pocket.

School work: Slow and Steady Wins this Race— REALLY!

Lesson 2

OBJECTIVE:

At the end of this lesson students will be able to

- Identify situations in which impulsivity interferes with schoolwork
- Recognize the benefits of utilizing impulse control to help with schoolwork
- Utilize impulse control techniques to help with schoolwork

MATERIALS NEEDED:

Pens/pencils, paper, candy, timer, and masking-tape

SCRIPT:

The role of student is one of the most important and difficult roles of adolescent life. School success is difficult enough without the added complications of poor impulse control. Though we may truly want to do well on our school assignments, and know how to do the work, we may experience impulses which make it tough to complete our work or difficult to "take our time" in order to do our work well. We may have the impulse to "hurry up" and get our work done so we can talk to our friends or do something more enjoyable. We may also have the impulse to not do our work at all because we don't like having to think so hard. By using impulse control we can learn to do better on our school work and make school a more enjoyable place to be.

RATIONALE:

Impulsive students make poorer grades than more reflective students (Gargallo, 1993). They often have difficulty completing assignments, following instructions, and producing work consistent with their intellect (Harris, et al, 2005). Research has shown that impulsive students have more difficulty across academic tasks, specifically, verbal, mathematical and spatial reasoning (Harris, et al, 2005; Nietfeld & Bosma, 2003; Roberts, 1979).

School success increases a student's self-esteem, peer status, future opportunities, and overall enjoyment of the education process. Because impulsivity may impede some teens' academic success it is important for them to be aware that the root of their academic frustration may be more about their impulsivity than their IQ. It is important for students to identify the areas of school performance that are affected by impulsivity and learn strategies that assist them in becoming more successful.

Indeed, the ability to manage impulses can reshape a student's entire learning experience. By learning techniques such as scanning the work, delaying gratification (Bembenutty, Hefer, and Karabeneck, S., 1998), considering consequences and benefits of study (Harris, et al, 2005; Miranda, Jarque, & Tarraga, 2006), students can have a less stressful, more productive, and more enjoyable school experience.

DISCUSSION QUESTIONS:

- What are some of the impulses you have when you are about to begin an assignment? What are some of the consequences for following these impulses? What are some of the benefits for taking your time and staying on task?
- What are some of the consequences you have received for not turning in your work or rushing through an assignment?
- How do you feel when you turn in an assignment that you have rushed through in order to move on to something more fun? How do you feel when you get the assignment back from your teacher?
- What are some things you can tell yourself to control your impulses while you are doing your schoolwork?

Activities:

Ask students to arrange chairs in a circle with one fewer chair than the number of students. Ask for a volunteer to begin in the center of the circle and instruct the remaining students to take a seat. The student in the center of the circle will begin the activity by describing a time when s/he acted on an impulse when working on a school assignment and how it resulted in negative consequences. Instruct the students in the circle who have had similar impulses to stand up and find another chair. The person in the center should take this opportunity to move into an open chair. A new person will be left in the center to continue the activity.

Invite students to come up in front of the group one at a time. Explain that you will be doing a role reversal. The student will be a teacher and the adult facilitator of the group will be the student. The situation is that the "teacher" has just given a long math assignment and the "student" is acting on her/his impulses (i.e. complaining, avoiding, talking, etc.). Following this role-play, ask the student to describe her/his experience as the teacher. Allow other students to also voice perceptions of the role-play. Then allow students to brainstorm ideas that would help control the impulse that was demonstrated.

After explaining and distributing a non-stimulating (boring) written activity (anything that will consume from 10-15 minutes of time, i.e. an essay, a question/answer sheet, etc.) explain to the students that self-monitoring is an important tool in increasing impulse control. Explain that during the time that students are working on their activity, they will be monitoring their on-task behaviors each time the timer buzzes (every 3 minutes) by writing "on-task" or "off-task" in the margin of the paper they are using for the activity. Explain to the students that if they are engaged in and actively working on the activity at the time that the timer goes off to write "on-task" and if they are thinking about or doing something other than the assignment to write "off-task." Set the timer to buzz every 3 minutes. Review the results at the conclusion of the activity comparing when most students were "on-task" and "off-task."

Place a long piece of masking tape on the floor at one end of the room to be a *Start* line. Then place another long piece of masking tape on the floor approximately 20 ft. away to be the *Finish* line. Ask students to line up, side-by-side, behind the *Starting* line. Then, one at time, ask students to name behaviors that are needed to be successful in school. Each time a students is able to identify a behavior, that student will take one giant step forward (no jumping). If a student is unable to name a behavior, s/he must stay in their current position. The fist student to cross the *Finish* line is the winner.

ACTIVITIES:

Prior to beginning this activity you will need to devise a list of steps to serve as a simple treasure map with some kind of "treasure" at the end. The steps should include clear instructions, (i.e. take three big steps forward, take two steps to your right, walk forward to the waste basket, turn in a complete circle, and reach under the desk, etc.) Bringing in one or two students at a time, read the directions out loud and ask students to write down the steps as you read them. Then direct them to follow their written directions to see if they can find the "treasure." (The treasure can be a piece of candy or some other small prize.)

Instruct students to take a piece of paper and a pencil and to write on the paper exactly what the facilitator verbally describes. Remind them that they must listen very carefully because the instructions will only be given one time. If they listen and follow instructions exactly, they will be able to identify the object that they have drawn. Instructions can be given for any letter, number or basic shape and should be given very slowly and deliberately.

- The instructions for making the number 4 are as follows: "In the middle of the page, draw a straight two (2) inch line that goes up and down on the page; from the middle of that line draw a one inch line that goes to the left; from the middle of the first line draw a one inch line that goes to the right; and from the left end of the second line draw a one inch line that goes up. What do you have?"

How To Use Reproducible Sheets:

Reproducible Worksheet 2.1

Get to Know Your Impulses, allows students to identify various impulses which they may feel during various tasks in the classroom. Predicting impulsive behaviors can be helpful in controlling them when they arise.

> **Talk about it.** Discuss the impulses that students have identified. Ask if they see any patterns in their impulses and which seem most problematic.

Reproducible Worksheet 2.2

The Road to Success, allows students to identify consequences and benefits associated with acting or not acting on impulses to be lazy about participating in a work group. Impulses are not always about acting out; impulses can also be about avoiding tasks.

> **Talk about it.** Ask students whether short term or long term consequences and benefits were easier to imagine. Discuss the benefits of thinking about both; discuss how learning to control our impulses can help us to be successful on down the road.

Reproducible Worksheet 2.3

Slow your Roll, allows students to experience the importance of taking their time when completing assignments. If they rush through this worksheet they will miss an important step.

> **Talk about it.** Ask what would have happened had they worked too fast and not read carefully. Discuss the techniques used to "slow their roll" while following the directives of the worksheet. Discuss the benefits of working in a more cautious manner.

Reproducible Worksheet 2.4

Cheer Yourself on, allows students to identify positive self-talk from negative self-talk in controlling impulses during the school day. Impulsive youth do not have good internalized speech so teaching them to use positive self-talk is a helpful intervention.

> **Talk about it.** Discuss other positive statements that could be used to decrease impulsive behaviors related to schoolwork.

Reproducible Worksheet 2.5

Searching for Impulse Control, gives students the opportunity to complete a word search activity with positive and negative phrases associated with impulse control and school work.

> **Talk about it.** Discuss any questions that students have about the terms in the worksheet. Discuss strategies that the students used to stay on task while doing the wordsearch.

GET TO KNOW YOUR IMPULSES

Fill in the blanks with the impulse which you may be tempted with during similar situations.

Your teacher passes out a test at the beginning of class and tells you that you have until the end of the period to finish it. Your best friend is sitting behind you in class.

Impulse –

____

What could you tell yourself to fight off this impulse?

____

You have just begun a math assignment and in this class when you are finished you are allowed to use the computers in the back of the class.

Impulse –

____

What could you tell yourself to fight off this impulse?

____

Your teacher has just assigned a reading assignment and you are really excited to get to lunch and see your friends. Lunch doesn't start for 30 minutes.

Impulse –

____

What could you tell yourself to fight off this impulse?

____

THE ROAD TO SUCCESS

Read the situation below and list two possible consequences for acting on the impulse. Then list two possible benefits or rewards for using impulse control. Try to consider one future and one immediate consequence and benefit.

Your fourth hour teacher hands out a group history assignment that you are allowed to work in with a group of three other students. You stayed up late last night and are very tired. One of the students in your group "always" gets her work done so you know she will probably look up all of the answers even if you don't participate, but the teacher will know that she did most of the work. You have an impulse to lay your head on the desk and let the other students in your group complete the assignment.

If I follow through with the impulse :

(immediate consequence)

____

____

(future consequence)

____

____

If I don't follow through with the impulse :

(immediate consequence)

____

____

(future consequence)

____

____

Slow Your Roll

Taking your time to carefully read instructions and complete school work is an important part of school success. Sometimes we have impulses to rush through assignments in order to move on to something more enjoyable which makes it easy to make mistakes. Read the list of directives carefully and do what they tell you to do.

1. **Stand up.**
2. **Sit down.**
3. **Stand up.**
4. **Do five jumping-jacks.**
5. **Sit down.**
6. **Stand up.**
7. **Turn in a complete circle.**
8. **Sit down.**
9. **Stand up.**
10. **Clap three times.**
11. **Sit down.**
12. **Say your full name.**
13. **Stand up.**
14. **Snap your fingers three times.**
15. **Sit Down.**
16. **Stand up.**
17. **Turn in a complete circle.**
18. **Sit down**

Great Job. You are done. Do not complete the rest of the tasks.

19. **Stand up.**
20. **Sing "I'm a little Tea Pot" with all of the motions.**
21. **Sit Down.**

THE END

What did you do to help follow the directions and stay on task?

Cheer Yourself On

Draw an "**X**" through examples of self-talk which may cause you to act impulsively and circle examples of self-talk which may help you to control your impulses.

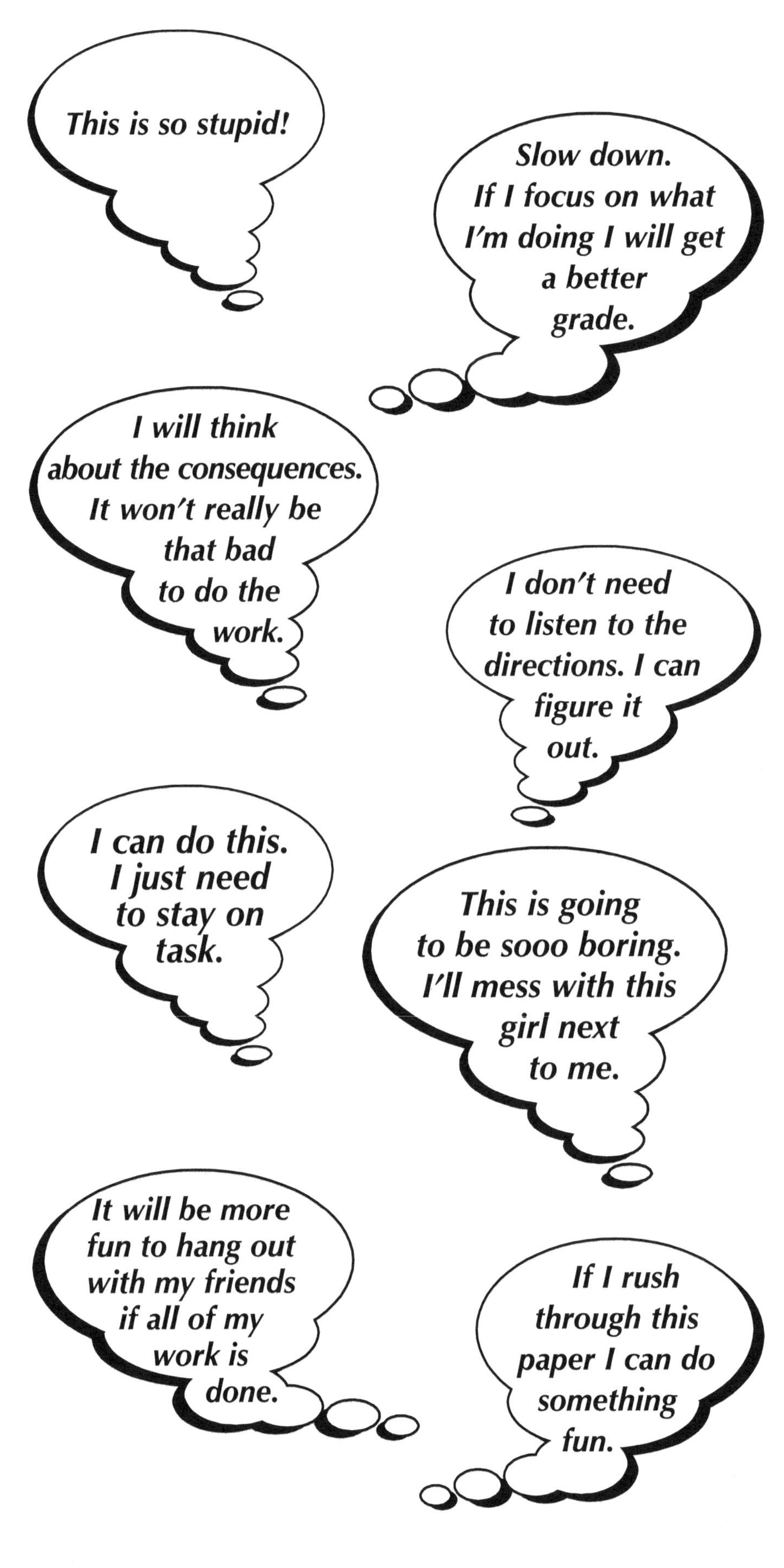

SEARCHING FOR IMPULSE CONTROL

Find and circle each word provide in the word bank.

CONSEQUENCES DELAY GRATIFICATION FOCUS
IMPULSE NEGATIVE TALK POSITIVE TALK
REWARDS RUSH SLOW DOWN
STOP AND THINK

D	F	C	Q	R	U	O	E	P	S	O	N	S	P	F	A	R	U	R	W
P	E	U	J	B	E	P	H	R	X	E	C	E	P	O	Z	K	N	Z	F
I	D	L	A	U	U	W	K	K	G	D	I	C	O	C	H	T	P	T	V
C	Z	L	A	L	L	L	A	A	U	L	I	N	S	U	L	D	P	R	H
N	F	Y	L	Y	D	E	T	R	R	P	W	E	I	S	P	X	Q	W	K
E	Z	U	I	R	G	I	B	Y	D	Z	Q	U	T	J	S	Q	X	J	Q
N	W	W	Z	A	V	R	S	P	M	S	W	Q	I	M	P	U	L	S	E
O	A	K	N	E	J	M	A	R	Y	Q	L	E	V	S	K	R	C	S	Y
X	F	E	T	N	O	E	Q	T	A	N	K	S	E	W	X	N	V	W	N
Q	L	A	R	M	D	R	B	V	I	I	G	N	T	X	S	O	B	W	J
H	L	I	R	C	U	P	D	B	Q	F	B	O	A	T	N	K	O	O	E
K	T	R	G	S	V	X	C	G	D	H	I	C	L	I	H	D	V	V	K
K	N	I	H	T	D	N	A	P	O	T	S	C	K	J	W	C	B	T	H
P	Y	F	R	C	K	D	M	L	G	Y	Y	L	A	O	L	B	X	C	I
J	J	Y	K	N	E	Z	C	E	C	L	A	R	L	T	D	C	G	S	W
O	D	O	J	F	X	H	F	Y	D	K	Q	S	O	Y	I	R	F	Z	P
F	K	E	O	S	W	B	N	G	J	P	U	U	Q	J	B	O	O	X	F
C	F	Z	D	A	L	O	S	Q	W	S	H	D	Z	Q	V	Y	N	R	R
V	V	O	P	O	J	A	D	L	O	F	Q	V	Q	I	H	Y	J	I	E
A	G	O	X	U	J	B	H	H	B	R	N	Q	G	U	H	H	T	C	H

How did you stay on task while doing this worksheet?

Lesson 3

Problem Solving: PROBLEM? What PROBLEM?

OBJECTIVE:

At the end of this lesson students will be able to

- Brainstorm multiple solutions for problems
- Examine the benefits and drawbacks of potential solutions
- Recognize the generalizability of problem-solving strategies

MATERIALS NEEDED:

Dry erase board, markers, paper, pens or pencils, scissors, colored paper or card stock, a copy of Appendix A and a large ball (volleyball size)

SCRIPT:

Everyone encounters problems from time to time. We can experience problems with school work or with parents or with friends. Problems do not mean that you are a bad person. But, given that problems are a part of the human condition, it is important to know how to be a good problem-solver. Good problem-solvers use a five (5) step approach to tackling their problems. These steps are:

STEP 1: Name the problem
STEP 2: Brainstorm several solutions
STEP 3: Look at the pros and cons of each of the brainstormed solutions
STEP 4: Choose a solution and try it
STEP 5: Decide how the solution worked

RATIONALE:

Research shows adolescents who are good problem-solvers are more socially well adjusted (Mott & Krane, 1994). Yet impulsivity can be a barrier to learning problem-solving skills during childhood (McMurran, Blair, & Egan, 2002). Students who are impulsive do not take time to reflect on potential solutions to a problem; they make hasty responses without considering alternative behaviors. They are reactive to problems rather than reflective.

Good problem-solving skills increase flexibility, creativity, cooperation and self-esteem. And the good news is that numerous studies have shown that teaching problem solving skills helps to reduce impulsivity (Elias, Gara, Schuyler, Branden-Muller, & Sayette, 1991; Elias, & Weissberg, 1990; Gargallo, 1993).

DISCUSSION QUESTIONS:

- What kinds of problems do you encounter at home? In the classroom? With peers?
- How do you typically handle these kinds of problems?
- What makes a good problem-solver? Who do you know that you would consider a good problem-solver? Why?
- How does impulse control contribute to being a good problem-solver?

ACTIVITIES:

1

Write the five (5) step model for problem-solving described in the Script (above) down the left side of a blackboard/dry erase board. To the right of Step 1, write, "The zipper on your pants is broken." Then ask students to name 3-5 solutions for this problem (i.e. safety pin it, go home and change clothes, walk with a book in front of you the entire day, etc.). Write each solution in a horizontal line next to STEP 2. Then ask students to identify a "pro" and a "con" for each solution (i.e. for walking with book solution, the advantage could be that it saves time in that you don't have to really do anything to the zipper and the disadvantage could be that your hand would get tired of holding a book in place). Put each "pro" and "con" under its solution and next to STEP 3. Then ask students to consider all of the information that they have produced and to select which solution they would try. Then discuss how one could evaluate this solution.

Ask students to sit in a circle. One at a time, ask for volunteers to sit in the "Hot Seat" (a seat in the middle of the circle). Ask the person in the "Hot Seat" to share a problem tha s/he is having currently or has had in the past. Instruct the remaining students in the circle to *stop* and *think* of a potential solution for the problem. One at a time, have students share their solution with the person in the "Hot Seat." Instruct persons in the "Hot Seat" to refrain from criticizing the solution and to simply say, "Thank you for your idea" after hearing each one. Continue asking for volunteers to sit in the "Hot Seat" until everyone who wants a turn has had a turn.

Explain to students that there are four basic rules to brainstorming:

1. Think of as many solutions as possible
2. Do not criticize anyone's idea
3. Go for "out of the box" ideas
4. Consider combined and improved ideas on previously mentioned ideas

Then divide them up into groups of 3-4 students. Give each group paper and a pen or pencil. Tell them that you will be setting a timer and giving them five (5) minutes to come up with *as many* ideas as possible for some problems. Use some of the following problems or create your own:

- Someone keeps putting graffiti on your school's entryway
- There is a lot of racial tension in your school
- Your school's cafeteria food is really disgusting
- Your school is getting rid of its art program and many students are quite gifted in art

---

Using Appendix A, photocopy the solution cards onto colored paper (cardstock is better but any colored paper will do). Then cut them out and place them in a pile. Ask students to take turns drawing a card and giving a "pro" and "con" for the solutions printed on it. If students have difficulty coming up with ideas, inform them that they can ask for assistance from their peers.

Activities:

Direct students to stand in a large circle with someone holding a large ball (volleyball size). Ask the person holding the ball to state a *problem* (preferably a real problem but it could also be an imagined problem) and then call out another student's name while throwing the ball to her/him. That student must then catch the ball and suggest a solution to the problem; s/he then names another student and throws the ball to her/him. That student then tells what is positive about the solution and calls out a name and throws the ball to that student. That student then tells what is negative about the solution and calls out a name and throws the ball to that student. This sequence is repeated over and over with each throw of the ball: problem, solution, positive aspect of the solution, and negative aspect of the solution.

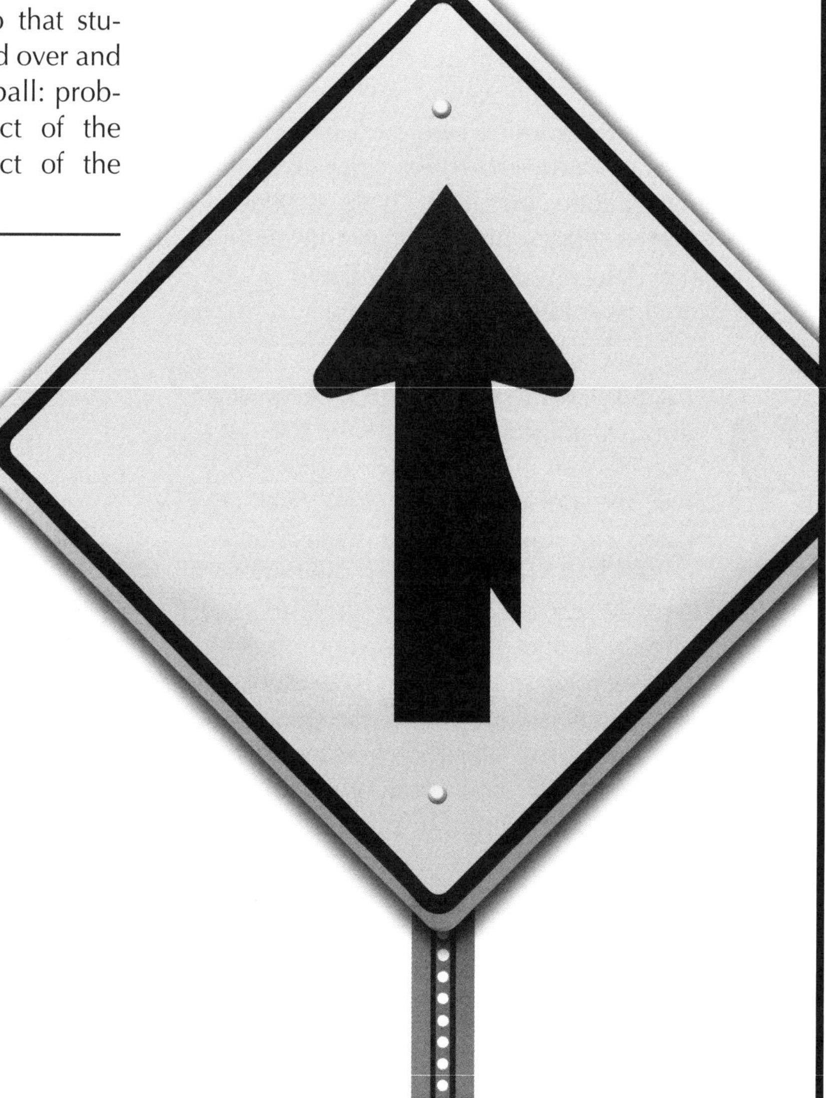

How To Use Reproducible Sheets:

Reproducible Worksheet 3.1

Rating My Problem-solving, asks students to assess various aspects of being a good problem-solver such as being able to brainstorm ideas, keeping "cool" when faced with problems, seeking the advice of others and making sure that everyone is happy with the outcome. It then asks students to identify their strengths and weaknesses regarding these components of problem-solving.

> **Talk about it.** Ask students to discuss their strengths and weaknesses from the worksheet. Encourage them to describe what kinds of specific actions they can take to improve their weak areas.

Reproducible Worksheet 3.2

Identify the Problem, shows students scenarios where there are two or more problems embedded in a given situation. They are asked to identify the problems and determine which problem needs to be worked on first.

> **Talk about it.** Ask students how they were able to decide which problem to work on first. Discuss the criteria that they used in coming to these conclusions.

Reproducible Worksheet 3.3

Brainstorming, allows students to brainstorm several solutions to a typical classroom problem. The page is organized in a mind-mapping structure so that students see the nonlinear fashion in which brainstorming takes place.

> **Talk about it.** Ask students to share their solutions from the worksheet. Discuss the pros and cons of each solution.

Reproducible Worksheet 3.4

What do I Need?, lets students examine several problems which have implied needs in them. They are asked to match the problems with expressive and instrumental "need-meeting" supports. More than one support can be matched with a problem.

> **Talk about it.** Discuss the needs that we have as humans. Ask students if problems have needs attached to them and how we can figure out what it is that we need in a given situation.

Reproducible Worksheet 3.5

Problem-solve This, gives students an opportunity to identify an individual problem and then asks them to generate three (3) solutions, examine the pros and cons of each solution, and to choose a solution. This worksheet can be done individually or in pairs.

> **Talk about it.** Ask students what their impulsive response would have been to their stated problem. Discuss how the problem-solving process improves outcomes.

Rating My Problem-Solving

Read each item and rate yourself by checking either "Absolutely" if it is absolutely true of you, "Sort of" if it is sort of true of you and "Not so much" if it is not true of you.

	Absolutely	Sort of	Not so much
1. I feel good about my problem solving abilities.	❑	❑	❑
2. When faced with a problem, I like to think of lots of ideas to solve it.	❑	❑	❑
3. When faced with a problem, I keep my cool.	❑	❑	❑
4. When faced with a problem, I like to seek advice from others more knowledgeable than myself.	❑	❑	❑
5. When faced with a problem, I don't let myself feel pressured to come up with a quick answer.	❑	❑	❑
6. When faced with a problem, I feel energized about an opportunity to be creative.	❑	❑	❑
7. When faced with a problem, I try to make sure that the outcome is positive for everyone.	❑	❑	❑
8. Others recognize me as a good problem-solver.	❑	❑	❑

Now go back and put a star by the item that you are best at and circle the one that you most need to work on.

IDENTIFY THE PROBLEM

Listed are scenarios which have at least two problems embedded in them. Identify both problems and then decide which one you would work on first.

Jared was going to P.E. one day. He knew that they were going to play basketball and he was really looking forward to it. When he got to his locker, he saw that someone had broken into it and stolen his gym shorts. He became so angry that he slammed the locker door shut and began cursing and accusing the people around him of being thieves.

PROBLEM 1:

____

____

PROBLEM 2:

____

____

PROBLEM TO BE ADDRESSED FIRST:

____

____

Latisha was having a hard time in algebra. She was confused and lost most of the time in class but she was too embarrassed to ask for help. She gave up on trying to do her homework and so her grade soon fell to an 'F.'

PROBLEM 1:

____

____

PROBLEM 2:

____

____

PROBLEM TO BE ADDRESSED FIRST:

____

____

Brain-Storming

Look at the problem in the circle in the middle of the page. Think of as many solutions as you can. Write them in the circles that surround the problem. If you need more circles, feel free to draw them in.

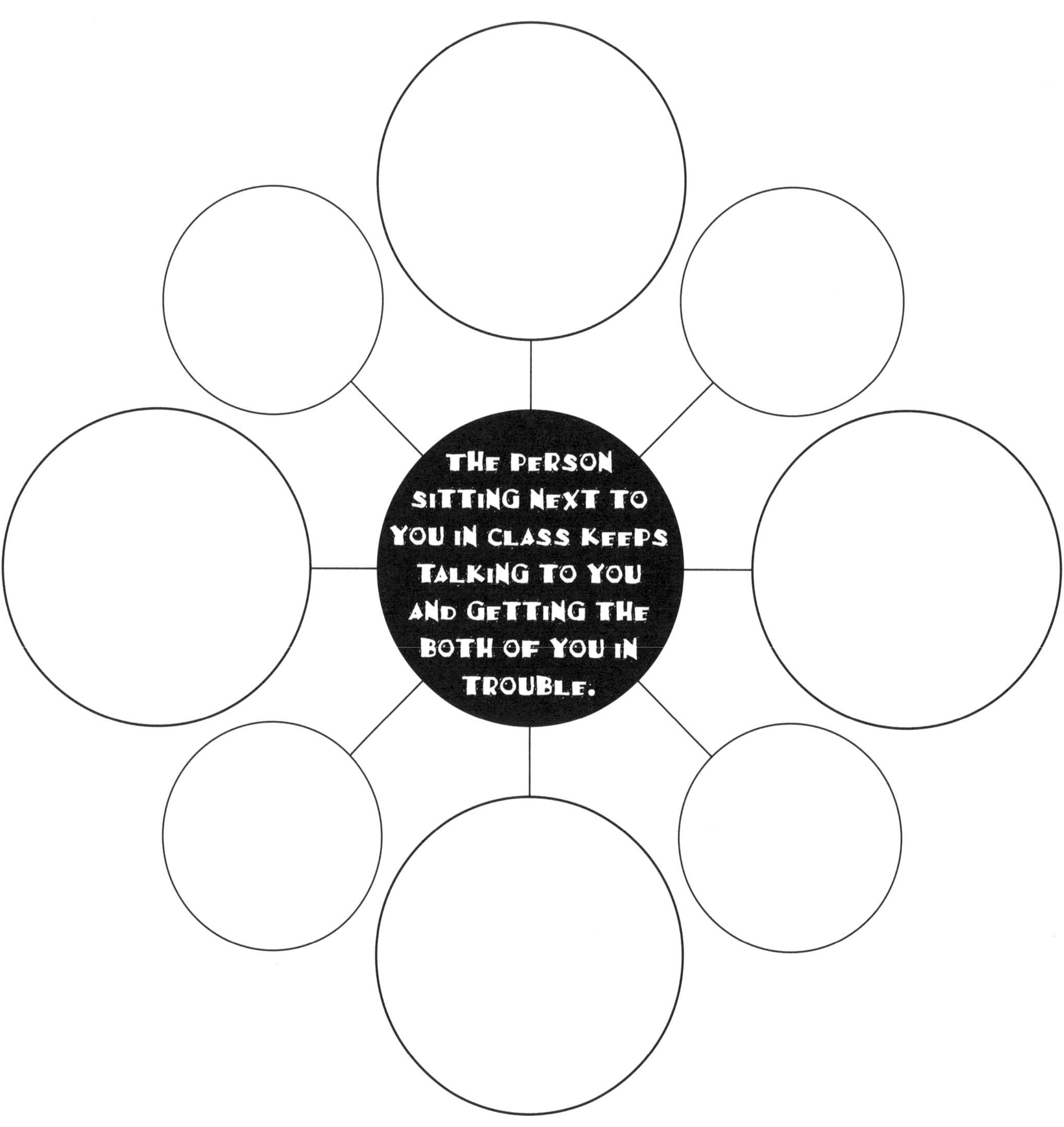

THE PERSON SITTING NEXT TO YOU IN CLASS KEEPS TALKING TO YOU AND GETTING THE BOTH OF YOU IN TROUBLE.

What Do I Need?

Listed on the left side of the page are several problems that teens face. Listed on the right side of the page are several resources. Match problems on the left to the resources on the right by drawing a line to connect them. A problem may need more than one resource so feel free to draw several lines from a single problem.

Problems	Resources
Carmetta can't find her geography book.	Emotional support
Ricky's parents are getting a divorce.	Personal power
Bailey's boyfriend just broke up with her.	Advice
Mekada keeps sleeping through her alarm in the mornings.	Money
Jeremy ruined one of his friend's video games.	More rest
Cynde keeps hearing a group of girls make fun of her when she walks.	Stress Management
Jason is making a failing grade in English.	Assistance with the task
Anna sees her best friend cheating on the math test.	Courage

Problem-Solve This

Identify the Problem:

Think of Several Solutions:

Examine the Pros and Cons of the Solutions:

PROs	CONs

PROs	CONs

PROs	CONs

Choose a Solution and Try It:

Decision-making: Decisions, Decisions, Decisions

Lesson 4

Objective:

At the end of this lesson students will be able to

- Identify the importance of being able to make informed, well considered decisions
- Recognize the future implications of certain kinds of decisions
- Use impulse control techniques to help make better decisions
- Understand how to use a cost/benefit analysis to make decisions

Materials Needed:

Pens/pencils, paper, chalk/dry-erase board, and chalk/dry-erase markers

Rationale:

Adolescents face daily decisions that can have serious future implications. Adolescents tend to make decisions that are riskier than adults, and impulsive adolescents make even riskier decisions that the average adolescent. Indeed, impulsive teens may not consider the risks involved in a particular decision and be overly optimistic about their abilities to avoid dangerous situations. They may have a hard time examining the possible consequences of certain decisions or be overly influenced by emotions in decision-making (Fischhoff, 1992; Ganzel, 1999). Problems with delayed gratification can also negatively influence decision making, as can peer influences (Gardner & Steinberg, 2005).

Good decision-making requires the ability to consider many factors. This is often difficult for impulsive youth as it is calls for slowing down to gather additional information, and taking time to examine possibilities.

Script:

We make many decisions each day. Some decisions are easy to make and there is really no "bad" choice, like deciding what we want to eat for breakfast or what socks to wear. Other choices are more difficult to make and sometimes these choices have serious consequences and can affect our lives for a long time. These, more important decisions require a little more thought and planning. It is important that we carefully look at options and consider all of the information available about these decisions. Certain choices can influence our opportunities and experiences for the rest of our lives so it is very important that we do not act impulsively. By using impulse control we can take our time and think through decisions making choices that we can feel proud of.

Discussion Questions:

- What is a decision you have made recently? What did you think about before you made it?
- What are some of the things that you consider when you make a decision? Do you always consider the different choices that you have?
- What makes one decision more important than another? What is a decision that you have made that did not affect your future?
- How did you decide what to wear today? What did you have to consider to make this decision (i.e. weather, what was clean, if it fit, how it felt, etc.)?
- What is a decision that you made that has affected your future?
- Can you think of a time when you made a good decision that paid off for you later on down the road? What kinds of things did you think about before making that decision? Did you make the decision quickly or did you take your time and think it through?

Activities:

1

Ask students to sit in a circle. One at a time, ask students to sit in the middle of the circle (the "Hot Seat"). Ask the student in the Hot Seat to discuss a decision that s/he is currently being faced with. Allow the students in the circle to respond by completing the statement, " If that were my decision I would need to consider __________". Allow time for discussion if needed.

Ask students: "What electives (i.e. band, football, cheer, academic team) will you choose to take this year?" Ask how this might be an important decision. Ask what electives they have chosen in the past and what criteria they used to make the decision. Review the concept of "delayed gratification," explaining that just because a choice seems easiest or most fun it may not be the best choice.

Explain to students that good decision making considers the impact that the decision may have on their future. The more impact on your future the more carefully one should examine possible choices. At the top of a dry erase board write *"Will you go to a high school party where there will be no parents?"* Ask students to consider future implications of attendance at the party. Under the question, write "Attend" and "Don't Attend." Under each of these headings write benefits/consequences for the next day, the next month, in five (5) years. Here is an example:

"Will you go to a high school party where there will be no parents?"

	Attend	
	Benefits	**Consequences**
Next day:		
Next month:		
In 5 years:		

	Don't Attend	
	Benefits	**Consequences**
Next day:		
Next month:		
In 5 years:		

Explain to students that an important part of making good decisions is gathering more information about the situation. Provide each student with a piece of paper and a pencil and ask students to draw a fist sized circle in the center of the sheet and to draw a dog in the circle. Then read out loud, "Your parents tell you that you can get a puppy but you will have to be responsible for all of the duties that go along with having a pet, including paying for its shots." Then ask students to think about any additional information that would be necessary to make the best decision. Direct them to write these down around the outside of the circle (mind-mapping). When everyone has completed their sheet ask students to share with the group what they have written. Discuss where they could go to get the additional information that they thought was necessary. Other decisions that can be used in this exercise include where to go to college, whether or not to join a sports team, what kind of new stereo system to purchase, what to do in the summer, etc.

ACTIVITIES:

Write the following list of decisions on the dry erase board and go through each one. Read each decision aloud and ask students to either reply "now", if the decision will not have long term consequences or "stop and think" if the decision is more complex and may affect their future. After students have identified the importance of the decision, allow them to discuss how they made the decision and what additional information, if any, is needed.

Decisions

- What will I wear to school today?
- Should I get my nose pierced?
- Should I go to summer camp?
- Will I have toast or cereal for breakfast?
- Will I skip school and hang out with my friend who is faking being sick?

How To Use Reproducible Sheets:

Reproducible Worksheet 4.1

Piece of Cake, allows students to look at different kinds of decisions and to rate how much research/thought they would put into making those decisions. Obviously some decisions are easy to make with very little thought or information-gathering needed. However, other decisions need more time to gather data and consider alternative choices.

> **Talk about it.** Ask students to report what criteria they used to mark each item (i.e. how it might effect the future, how much it fit their value systems, etc.)

Reproducible Worksheet 4.2

Sooo Many Choices, provides students with the opportunity to brainstorm an array of choices for a particular decision. Students are asked to read the situation in the center of the sheet and to fill in the surrounding circles with possible choices.

> **Talk about it.** Ask students to discuss what made a choice easy or difficult and if more easy choices or difficult choices seemed to be "right" choices.

Reproducible Worksheet 4.3

Which Path to Take, allows students to consider the future implications of making certain decisions by projecting what impact that decision may have on their lives at different times in the future. This activity allows students to consider both short term future impacts and long term future impacts.

> **Talk about it.** Discuss how thinking about the future might affect decision-making.

Reproducible Worksheet 4.4

Now and Later, allows students to respond to three (3) scenarios where they can take a look short term vs. long term benefits of particular decisions. Again, this allows students to consider more than just the "here and now" feeling.

> **Talk about it.** Ask students if the easiest choices were the best choices in the long term. Discuss how students would handle each of the situations if they decided to make a decision that would be better for the long term.

Reproducible Worksheet 4.5

Don't Forget Your Dreams, allows students to examine their goals/values as criteria for making decisions. Students are asked to list some of their goals and dreams and then to brainstorm possible choices for dealing with a situation. They are then asked to consider how their choices fit with their goals and dreams.

> **Talk about it.** Ask students if it was helpful to frame their choices by whether or not they will help them achieve their goals. Discuss how a decision not to act on a situation is also a decision with it's own consequences.

Reproducible Worksheet 4.6

Is it Worth it, allows students to practice conducting a cost/benefits analysis of certain decisions. This process is similar to the formal process of Cost-Benefit analysis used in many corporations. It involves weighing the total expected costs against the total expected benefits of an action in order to make the best possible choice.

> **Talk about it.** Discuss the costs and benefits that students identified in each of the scenarios. Discuss how different students will identify different costs and benefits based on their values and personalities.

PIECE OF CAKE

Carefully read each situation below and rate the amount of time that you would need to gather information and consider your decision by placing an "X" in one of the three (3) columns.

	MINIMAL THOUGHT	MODERATE THOUGHT	A LOT OF THOUGHT
1. What movie should I rent when my friend stays the night?	❑	❑	❑
2. Should I tell my parents that I think my brother is smoking?	❑	❑	❑
3. What should I name my new pet bird?	❑	❑	❑
4. Should I tell the truth about breaking my mother's vase?	❑	❑	❑
5. What summer activities am I going to get involved with this year?	❑	❑	❑
6. Am I going to break up with my girl/boyfriend?	❑	❑	❑
7. What college should I go to?	❑	❑	❑
8. I know there will be alcohol at the party, am I going to try it?	❑	❑	❑
9. Will I wear a jacket to the game or not?	❑	❑	❑

Why is it important to recognize when a decision needs extra consideration?

____

Sooo Many Choices

Read the decision in the circle and brainstorm different choices that would be possible when making the decision and write the choices down in the empty circles. Then decide whether or not each choice would be an easy choice to make by circling the word "easy" or "difficult" under each brainstormed idea.

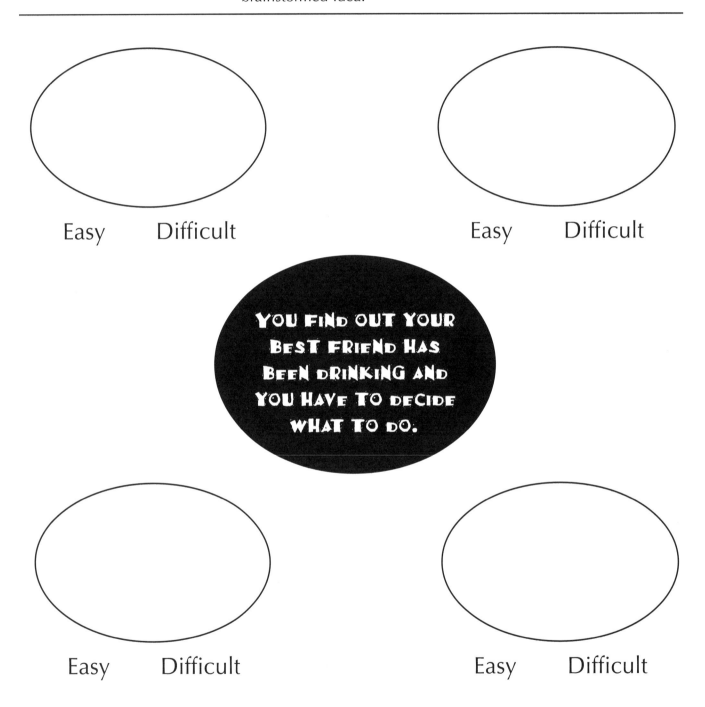

Easy Difficult

Easy Difficult

YOU FIND OUT YOUR BEST FRIEND HAS BEEN DRINKING AND YOU HAVE TO DECIDE WHAT TO DO.

Easy Difficult

Easy Difficult

Which choice do you think would be best for your friend? Was that an "easy" choice or a "difficult" choice?

Which Path To Take?

Read the dilemma and in the spaces provided, write down two different decisions that you might make. Then write down the affects of each decision at different times in your life.

Dilemma

You are struggling in your math class and your teacher suggests that you come in for tutoring. If you decide to participate in tutoring, you will be unable to hang out with your friends three afternoons per week. If you decide not to participate in tutoring, you may fail your math class.

CHOICE #1 ______________________________ ______________________________

CHOICE #2 ______________________________ ______________________________

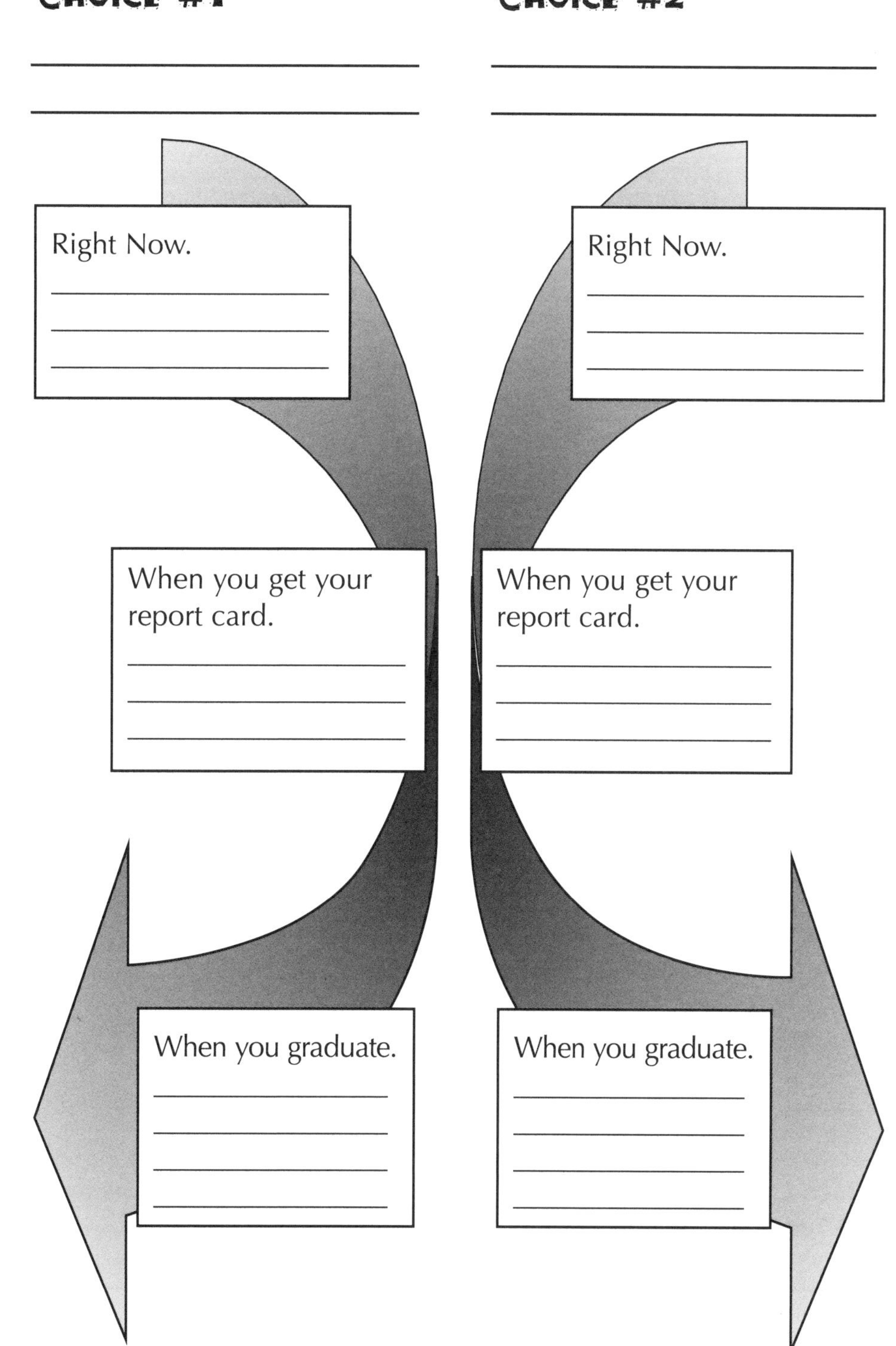

NOW AND LATER

Read each situation and write down a decision that would feel good now and a decision that would be better for the future.

---

1. You are hanging out with your friends and some of them think it would be fun to throw rocks at house windows. What do you do?

Decision that feels good now:

____

____

Decision that is good for the future:

____

____

2. You have plans to go to your friend's house and hang out on Saturday morning. On your way out the door your mom asks if you finished your chores. You have not finished your chores. What do you do?

Decision that feels good now:

____

____

Decision that is good for the future:

____

____

3. You are walking alone through the school parking lot and you find a wallet with $50.00 in it. What do you do?

Decision that feels good now:

____

____

Decision that is good for the future:

____

____

Don't Forget Your Dreams

List some of your goals and dreams in the box. Read the decision and write several choices that you could make then under each choice circle yes if that choice might help you achieve your goals and dreams and no if the choice may hurt your goals and dreams.

Decision: It is Friday night and you are grounded. Your parents have gone to bed early and you are the only one awake in the house. One of the kids down the street is having a party and everyone at school has been talking about it. His parents are out of town and you know there will be alcohol at the party. What are some of your choices?

CHOICE #1:

____

______________________ . Will this choice help you attain your goals? **YES** **NO**

CHOICE #2:

____

______________________ . Will this choice help you attain your goals? **YES** **NO**

CHOICE #3:

____

______________________ . Will this choice help you attain your goals? **YES** **NO**

CHOICE #4:

____

______________________ . Will this choice help you attain your goals? **YES** **NO**

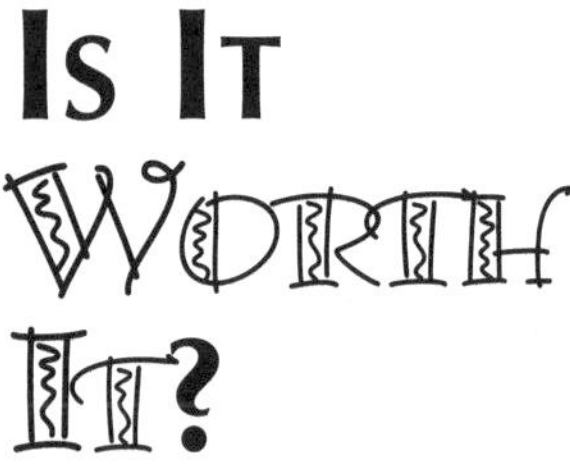

Count the Costs and Benefits.
List and compare the costs (problems or sacrifices) and benefits (advantages or gains) of making each of the following decisions.

Samantha decides to study hard and make good grades.

COSTS	BENEFITS

Thomas decides to make up a rumor about Enrique because they got in an argument at lunch.

COSTS	BENEFITS

Daryl decides to see a tutor because he is having trouble in math.

COSTS	BENEFITS

Rami decides to lie to his parents about adult supervision at a party he wants to go to.

COSTS	BENEFITS

Mood Management: Master of My Emotional Universe

Lesson 5

Objective:

At the end of this lesson students will be able to

- Identify cognitive distortions that lead to poor self-regulation
- Change unproductive self-talk to helpful self-talk
- Identify behavioral distractions in order to avoid rumination

Materials Needed:

Paper, pens or pencils, multiple copies of Appendix B, pictures of brains, scissors, two (2) hats or caps, and a CD player

Script:

All of us feel uncomfortable feelings from time to time. Things happen that cause us to feel sad or embarrassed or overwhelmed or discouraged. We may have those feelings without any reason at all. The question becomes, do these feelings control us or do we control them? Mood management means that we control our feelings through positive coping strategies. We learn to conquer our bad moods and uncomfortable feelings through talking to others, distraction, problem-solving and self-talk, rather than overeating, using drugs, having sex or cutting ourselves in order to feel better. Being emotionally healthy has great benefits, as well. People who cope with emotions and are emotionally healthy are more successful in life, have better relationships and do better in school!

Rationale:

Adolescence is a time of intense emotional arousal. Behavioral and cognitive processes mature in adolescence which enables them to regulate these intense emotions. Unfortunately for the impulsive adolescent, however, these processes appear to not take place. In fact, compared to other adolescents, impulsive teens appear to have *poorer* emotional regulation. They use fewer appropriate and greater inappropriate regulation strategies (d'Acremont & Van der Lindon, 2007; Silk, et. al., 2007). Impulsive youth tend to disengage, ruminate and/or engage in impulsive action when experiencing negative emotions, rather than problem-solve, distract, or use self-talk strategies. Because impulsive teens have difficulty coping with negative emotions they have less emotional intelligence, are less resilient, and are more prone to internalizing and externalizing behaviors (Ciarrochi, Chan, & Baigar, 2001; Silk, Steinberg, & Morris, 2003). Assisting impulsive teens in the development of mood management and emotional regulation strategies can be an effective contribution to overall adolescent adjustment and mental health.

Discussion Questions:

- Have you ever felt overwhelmed with your emotions? What was the situation? How did you cope?
- Who do you know who seems to cope well with negative situations and feelings? How do you think they do it?
- When is a time that you coped well with something? How did you do it?
- Why would someone want to learn how to manage their moods and feelings? Why do *you* want to?

ACTIVITIES:

1

Invite students to go on a Coping Skills Scavenger Hunt. Give each student pencil and paper and tell them that they will have a designated period of time (i.e. 15 minutes) to go around and ask as many adults as possible how they cope with negative events and uncomfortable feelings. Instruct them to write these down. Winners can be those students who (1) obtain the greatest number of coping skills and/or (2) interview the greatest number of adults.

Explain to students how cognitive distortions can cause us to feel worse about a situation than we need to. Then pass out the multiple copies of the list of Cognitive Distortions in Appendix B. Give an example of one of the distortions (i.e. Disqualifying the Positive: Someone makes an 'A' on an assignment but thinks, "No big deal. It was an easy assignment."). Then ask students to give examples of the other distortions. If appropriate, go back around and ask students to name specific times when they were very, very upset about something and which cognitive distortion they may have been operating under. Discuss ways that one can change these distortions.

Cut out one (1) light and one (1) dark picture of a brain and glue each one onto a different hat or cap. Explain that the light brained hat represents positive thinking and the dark brained hat represents negative thinking (or "stinkin' thinkin'"). Then ask for three (3) students to come to the front of the group. Two (2) of the students will use the hats and the third student will stand in between them. Say to the group, "This is <*name of student in the middle*> and the two sides of her/his brain." Then have the student in the middle describe a situation that was difficult (i.e. "I lost my math book"). Direct her/him to turn to the "dark side of his brain" (student with the dark picture of a brain) and hear what it has to say. Have the student with the dark brain say things that are negative about the situation (i.e. "You are really stupid to lose that. No one loses their books. You are probably really going to get in trouble.") Ask the student in the middle how s/he feels. Then tell her/him to turn her/his back on that "stinkin' thinkin'" and to "Listen to the other side of her/his brain" (student with the light picture of a brain). Have the student with the light brain say things that are more positive and reality-based about the situation (i.e. "Even though you lost your math book, that doesn't mean that you won't find it or be able to get another one. Everyone loses something sometime."). Again ask the student in the middle how s/he feels. Discuss the differences. Repeat this exercise so that everyone gets an opportunity to participate.

Explain to students the meaning of optimism. Then read the quotation by Helen Keller, "Optimism is the faith that leads to achievement. Nothing can be done without hope and confidence." Ask students what they think she meant.

Explain that music is sometimes a good way to calm ourselves when we feel upset or overwhelmed. Ask students to bring in tapes or CDs of songs that soothe them. Then play these for the students while they close their eyes to relax.

How To Use Reproducible Sheets:

Reproducible Worksheet 5.1

Benefits of Mood Control, asks students to unscramble letters in order to read three (3) of the benefits of mood control. They are: "You will feel better," "Other people will respect you," and "You will have a clearer mind."

Talk about it. Ask students if they can think of other benefits of being able to manage their moods and feelings. Discuss the idea that one can think more clearly when emotions are calm.

Reproducible Worksheet 5.2

Making Mountains out of Molehills, asks students to identify and write the names of the persons who are using magnification (or "making mountains out of molehills"). They are then asked to correct the thinking of persons with a more positive self-statement. "Making mountains out of molehills" is particularly problematic in adolescence so this is an important exercise in mood management.

Talk about it. Ask students to explain how they were able to identify "making mountains out of molehills" thinking. Discuss how this affects feelings.

Reproducible Worksheet 5.3

Stinkin' Thinkin', asks students to identify various types of cognitive distortions (or stinkin' thinkin'). Four types of cognitive distortions are presented: all-or-nothing thinking, jumping to conclusions, magnification, and disqualifying the positive.

Talk about it. Discuss how "stinkin' thinkin'" creates negative feelings. Ask students to identify times when they have used "stinkin' thinking.'" Go back to the worksheet and ask students to change each negative thought into a more realistic, positive thought.

Reproducible Worksheet 5.4

Thoughts ⟶ Feelings, presents two (2) different situations, each with two (2) different thoughts. Students are asked to write down the feeling that each thought would produce. This worksheet helps students understand how thinking affects emotions.

Talk about it. Ask students to compare the feelings that each thought produced. Ask whether or not they were surprised by how much a thought can change a feeling – even when the situation is the same. Discuss how students can use this information in their own lives.

Reproducible Worksheet 5.5

Distractions, presents a list of activities that students can engage in in order to distract themselves when feeling upset or overwhelmed. Distraction is a strategy that almost always works if utilized. Students are asked to circle their three (3) favorite distractions.

Talk about it. Ask students if they use any of these distraction techniques in order to soothe themselves. Ask them to describe which ones and in what circumstances they have found them to be effective.

Reproducible Worksheet 5.6

Dealing with It, presents students with three (3) situations where they would feel distressed in some way. They are asked to write down helpful self-talk and a self-soothing action/distraction for each situation.

Talk about it. Ask students to share any current situations from their own lives where the group could help them identify how to talk to themselves about it or how to self-sooth/distract themselves.

BENEFITS OF MOOD CONTROL

Unscramble the following phrases to find out some of the benefits of mood control:

(1) YUO LWLI EFEL TERTEB.

______ ______ ______ ______.

(2) ORTEH OEPPEL LIWL

______ ______ ______

PCSREET OUY.

______ ______.

(3) YUO LLWI VEHA

______ ______ ______

RAELREC DIMN.

______ ______.

Making Mountains Out of Molehills

Have you ever heard the expression, "Making mountains out of molehills?" Sometimes we magnify our situations and make them worse than they really are. Look at the situations below. Decide which kids have "made mountains out of molehills" and put their names at the bottom. Then write a more realistic way that each person could think about their situation.

Henry doesn't make the football team. He tells himself that he is a complete loser.

Kia breaks her mother's vase. She tells herself that it was an accident and that everyone has accidents now and then.

Charlene's best friend is angry with her. She tells herself that everyone has the right to their feelings and that as soon as her friend cools off she will talk to her about the problem.

Peter gets yelled at for coming home late from a friend's house. He tells himself that his mom is totally unfair and stupid.

Hajim does poorly on a math test. He tells himself that he can pull the overall grade up if he studies more.

Kids "making mountains out of molehills":

____

____

____

What do they need to say to themselves in order to feel better:

____

____

____

After reading the definitions of each of the various types of cognitive distortions (stinkin' thinkin'), identify the kind of stinkin' thinkin' that each thought bubble represents.

All-or-nothing thinking – Thinking of things in absolute terms, like "always", "every" or "never."

Jumping to conclusions – Assuming something negative where there is no evidence to support it (i.e. assuming the intents of others).

Magnification – Exaggerating the way people or situations truly are.

Disqualifying the positive – Continually negating or "shooting down" positive experiences.

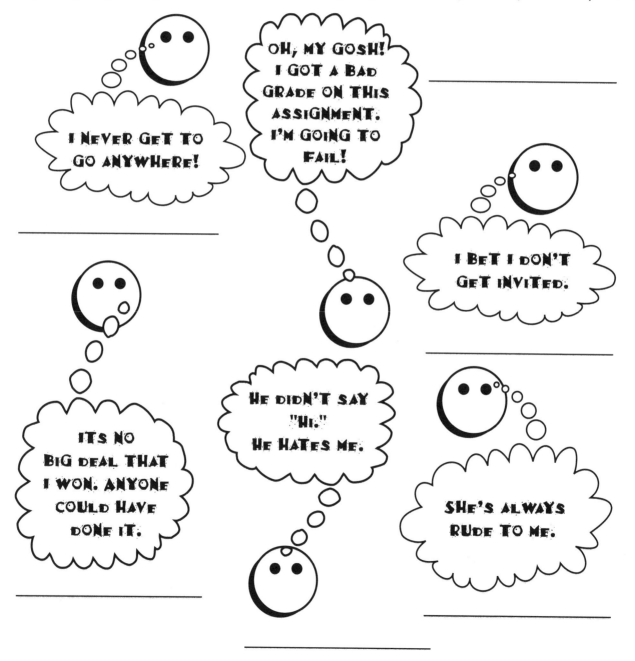

I NEVER GET TO GO ANYWHERE!

____

OH, MY GOSH! I GOT A BAD GRADE ON THIS ASSIGNMENT. I'M GOING TO FAIL!

____

I BET I DON'T GET INVITED.

____

ITS NO BIG DEAL THAT I WON. ANYONE COULD HAVE DONE IT.

____

HE DIDN'T SAY "HI." HE HATES ME.

____

SHE'S ALWAYS RUDE TO ME.

____

Thoughts → Feelings

Listed below are two (2) different situations, each with two (2) different attitudes (thoughts) about the situations. Write down how each of the thoughts would make you feel.

SITUATION:
Your brother broke one of your favorite CDs.

THOUGHT #1:
"He is *always* breaking my stuff. It's not fair."

FEELING:

THOUGHT #2:
"Well, I guess he is going to have to figure out a way to replace it."

FEELING:

SITUATION:
You have a ton of homework.

THOUGHT #1:
"Maybe we won't have as much tomorrow night."

FEELING:

THOUGHT #2:
"This is terrible. I'm not going to be able to do *any*thing tonight!"

FEELING:

Distractions

Teachers and parents usually tell you not to get distracted. However, when you are upset or overwhelmed, it is a good thing to distract yourself from your uncomfortable feelings. Read the distractions below and circle your three (3) favorite. Feel free to add some of your own.

Play a sport

Dance

Build something

Listen to music

Read

Garden

Call a friend

Go fishing

Ride a bike

Play an instrument

Clean/organize

Play video games

Cook or bake

Use the computer

Watch TV

Meditate

Pray

Draw

Write poetry

Write in a diary

Exercise

Run

Play with a pet

Lay on my bed and think of soothing places

Dealing with It

Everyone feels sad or disappointed sometimes. But there are things that you can do to help yourself feel better. Read the situations below. Then write down (1) what you could tell yourself and (2) what you could do in order to make yourself feel better.

Situation	Helpful self-talk	Self-soothing action/distraction
Your family had your pet dog since before you were born. You and the dog have always been especially close. However, he has gotten old and recently died.		
Several kids at school have been saying that you are stuck-up. They have started to leave you out of things.		
Your friend wants you to go to a really cool movie that you have been wanting to see for a long time but your mother says that you can't go.		

Lesson 6

Anxiety: Don't be a Worry Wart

Objective:

At the end of this lesson students will be able to

- Identify sources of anxious feelings
- Recognize and identify different types and levels of anxious feelings
- Utilize coping skills to reduce anxious feelings and help make it easier to use impulse control

Materials Needed:

Dry erase/chalk board, markers, pens/pencils, paper, a copy of Appendix C, scissors, and a container

Script:

Everyone feels anxious or nervous from time to time. We may be scared to speak in front of large groups of people or worried about doing poorly on a test; we may get nervous about going to the dentist or we may feel worried for reasons we can't really explain. When we are frightened or nervous we can be impulsive and act before thinking about the consequences. Some anxious feelings can be small and some can be great, but regardless of the level, it is important for us to be able to stop, calm down, and think before we act. When we show impulse control in anxious situations, it can help us to make decisions that we don't have to worry about getting in trouble for; decisions that won't cause us more anxiety.

Rationale:

Anxiety is another emotional state that can make it difficult to make decisions and think of consequences. Research has shown a positive correlation between impulsivity and higher levels of anxiety (Weinberger, 1997). Similar to anger, anxiety affects the more primitive (old) part of the brain where higher levels of cognitive functioning are not available, making it difficult for students to stop, think, and make intelligent decisions.

Everyone has fears and many of these can be real. Fears of real threats serve to protect against harmful situations. It is when fears become excessive or irrational that one may find himself using impulsive, ineffective problem solving techniques. It is important for anxious youth to be able to stop and relax prior to beginning problem-solving or decision-making. This enables them to rationally consider the consequences of their future actions free of the influence of anxiety. Conversely, children acting in an impulsive manner tend to find themselves in anxiety inducing situations as a result of their behavior, ever perpetuating the anxiety/impulsivity cycle. For this reason it is important to address this problem from both sides.

Discussion Questions:

- What situations cause you to feel nervous? What situations cause you to feel worried?
- What ways do you try to relax when you are feeling anxious or scared?
- What are some of the impulses that you have when you are worried, nervous or scared?
- What are some of the ways you can control your impulses when feeling nervous or scared?

Activities:

1

Ask willing students to describe a situation in which they might experience anxious feelings (i.e. nervous, worried, scared etc.). Then ask them to describe in detail the feelings that they experience during the situation and to show with their bodies how the anxiety shows itself (biting of fingernails, nervous look on face, shaking, etc.). While the student is physically acting out the anxiety, direct the other students to speak out ideas of positive self-talk that the student could use (i.e. "This will be over soon", "I know it seems bad now, but everything will be OK", etc.).

Explain to students that people feel different levels of anxiety even when experiencing similar situations. Write the following levels of anxious feelings on a dry-erase/chalk board with accompanying directions:

No anxious feelings – remain seated
A little nervous – raise one hand
Very nervous – raise two hands
Worried – stand up
Scared - stand up and raise one hand
Terrified – stand up and raise both hands

Then read the following list of anxiety producing situations and ask students to identify which level of anxiety they would experience and to follow the directions on the board. Encourage students to be honest and not to feel like they have to feel exactly like others would feel.

- Your teacher asks you to read a paragraph in front of the class.
- You are about to begin a math test.
- Your grandparent is in the hospital.
- Your pet has run away and been gone for two days.
- Your best friend is angry with you.
- Your boyfriend/girlfriend has broken up with you.
- You are riding a very high roller coaster and going up the first big incline.
- You walk through a spider web.

Ask students to give examples of situations which cause "low levels" of anxiety and situations which cause "high levels" anxiety. Ask students to explain what kind of feelings they experience with the different levels of anxious feelings (i.e. nervous, worried, scared, terrified, etc.) and what impulses (i.e. run away, be silent, yell, etc.) might accompany the anxious feelings.

Explain to students that using relaxation techniques can be a helpful way to reduce anxiety. Ask students to tense one arm and to focus on the tension and to hold it for three (3) seconds. Then direct them to immediately relax the tension and to focus on the relaxed state of the arm. Do this repeatedly with different body parts. Discuss how this relaxation technique can be used when experiencing anxious feelings.

Ask students to draw a picture of one of their most anxiety producing situations. When complete, ask them to turn the picture upside down and see if it resembles something funny or interesting. Then ask students to add more detail to the upside down picture, creating a humorous version. Explain to students that they can do a mental version of this activity any time they experience feelings of anxiety.

Copy and cut out the anxiety producing situations from Appendix C. Place situations in a container; then direct students to each pick one. One by one, ask students to read their situations and then state the kinds of calming self-talk that they would use to make themselves feel better in that specific situation.

How To Use Reproducible Sheets:

Reproducible Worksheet 6.1

The Many Faces of Anxiety, allows students to describe various situations that provoke different states and degrees of anxiety. This worksheet assists students in building a vocabulary of anxious feelings and identifying situations that produce them.

Talk about it. Ask students to identify additional words related to anxiety (i.e. edgy, jumpy, panicky, uneasy, etc.). Discuss some of the situations that they described on the worksheet.

Reproducible Worksheet 6.2

Rate Your Anxiety, allows students to rate levels of anxiety in various anxiety-producing situations. They are asked to use a Likert scale.

Talk about it. Ask students to discuss which anxiety-producing situations produces the most stress for them and why. Discuss why it is important to be aware of situations that cause us the greatest levels of anxiety.

Reproducible Worksheet 6.3

Pick a Winner, allows students to use a four step process to calm themselves and use good judgment when responding to anxiety-producing situations. The four (4) steps are identifying the feeling, identifying the impulse, using soothing self-talk and making a good decision.

Talk about it. Discuss the four step process and how each step contributes to healthy/productive behaviors.

Reproducible Worksheet 6.4

Talking Yourself Down, allows students to consider self-talk as a way of coping with anxiety. Students are asked to identify positive self-talk statements by circling them and to identify negative self-talk statements by drawing an "X" through them.

Talk about it. Discuss which self-talk statements students have used in the past or which statements they might use in the future to reduce anxious feelings.

Reproducible Worksheet 6.5

Learning How to Cope, allows students to match various coping techniques to anxiety-producing situations. There are no correct answers here – simply what each student decides would work best for her/him.

Talk about it. Discuss why students found certain techniques to be helpful and others not to be helpful.

The Many Faces of Anxiety

There are many words to describe different types of anxious feelings. Write down the situations that cause the different kinds of anxiety listed below.

NERVOUS

____

____

____

WORRIED

____

____

____

SCARED

____

____

____

HORRIFIED

____

____

____

CONCERNED

____

____

____

Situations in which we experience higher levels of anxiety put us at a greater risk of acting impulsively, so it is important for us to be aware of what kinds of situations make us the most anxious. Check the box on the scale that corresponds to level of anxiety you would experience in each situation.

	No Anxiety	Little Anxiety	Some Anxiety	A Lot of Anxiety	Extreme Anxiety
1. You cut your hand and have to go the hospital for stitches.	❑	❑	❑	❑	❑
2. Your math teacher asks you to do a problem on the board in front of the class.	❑	❑	❑	❑	❑
3. You are on your way to your first day at a new school.	❑	❑	❑	❑	❑
4. You are participating in an Outdoor Challenge and it is your turn to climb onto the high wire that is 30 feet off the ground.	❑	❑	❑	❑	❑
5. You are home alone and the electricity goes out, leaving you in the dark.	❑	❑	❑	❑	❑

Pick a Winner

Using the four step process of (1) Recognize the feeling, (2) Identify the impulse, (3) Talk to yourself in a soothing manner, and (4) Choose an appropriate course of action, read the following situations and come up with the best choice.

You are hanging out with a group of friends and someone gets angry at you and begins to shout and shove you.

STEP 1: What do you feel?

STEP 2: What is your impulse?

STEP 3: Soothing self-talk.

STEP 4: What is your course of action?

2 **Your teacher asks you to read a difficult paragraph in front of the class.**

STEP 1: What do you feel?

STEP 2: What is your impulse?

STEP 3: Soothing self-talk.

STEP 4: What is your course of action?

TALKING YOURSELF DOWN

Positive self-talk is a helpful technique to calm yourself. Circle the examples of positive self-talk and place an "X" through examples of negative self-talk.

Identify the coping skill on the right that would be helpful to you for each of the stressful situations on the left. Draw a line to connect them. Coping skills may be used more than once.

Stressful situations	Coping skills
You hear a rumor about yourself	Take 5 deep breaths
You get a bad report card	Consider options
You get in an argument with one of your friends	Use positive self-talk
A big dog looks like it might attack you	Exercise
You break your mom's favorite bowl	Tense and relax body parts
Your best friend is in the hospital	Talk about it
You get called to the principal's office	

Lesson 7

Anger: Is Temper-Taming anything like Lion-Taming?

Objective:

At the end of this lesson students will be able to

- Identify situations which may lead to anger
- Better recognize the progression of arising anger
- Exercise impulse control when angry feelings arise

Rationale:

Aristotle once said "Anyone can become angry—that is easy. But to be angry with the right person, to the right degree, at the right time, for the right purpose and in the right way---this is not easy." Adolescence, in most cultures, is a period characterized by an increase in impulsive and aggressive behaviors, including anger. One of the most difficult times to practice impulse control (even for nonimpulsive students) is when anger arises.

Anger often acts as a barrier, making it difficult to problem-solve and address issues (Susman, et.al., 1987; Hanna & Hunt, 1999). There are many different "triggers" for anger and these vary from person to person. This chapter will assist students in identifying their anger triggers, recognizing the warning signs associated high levels of anger, and developing techniques to control angry impulses.

Materials Needed:

Pens/pencils, paper, chalk/dry-erase board, chalk/dry-erase markers, a copy of Appendix D, scissors, and a container

Script:

Anger is normal. Everyone experiences it now and then. However, some of us may become angry more often than we want to. Anger may even be getting us into trouble. We may feel angry if someone takes something that is ours; we may feel angry if someone says something to embarrass us; we may feel angry "just because." It is important for us to recognize our anger triggers, so that we can control our angry impulses. Controlling angry impulses helps us make better choices and take control of ourselves.

Discussion Questions:

- What are some of the things that make you the angriest? What was the last thing that you got really angry about?
- What are some of the impulses you have when you become angry?
- How do you feel after you have calmed down from being really angry? How do you think the people around you feel?
- How do you know that you are becoming angry? How does your body feel? What do you think about?
- What are some things you can do to control your impulses when you feel yourself becoming angry?

ACTIVITIES:

1

Explain to students that it is important to be able to regain control of oneself during an anger episode. Ask each student to pretend to be very angry (i.e. putting an angry expression on her/his face, tightening muscles, clenching fists, raising voice, etc.) for approximately 10 seconds. Ask the students to regain control of their anger as quickly as possible after the ten second anger outburst. Give each student an opportunity to explain what they did to regain control of their anger.

Ask each student to describe an experience that made them, or could make them, extremely angry and to explain the impulse(s) that accompanied or would accompany the anger. Ask the rest of the students to say "Stop and Think!" at the end of each impulse. Then ask the participating student to state the possible consequence(s) for acting on the impulse.

Give each student a pen or pencil and a piece of paper. Ask the students to draw a stick figure in center of the paper. Explain that when someone begins to feel angry that their body changes; different areas of the body become tense or agitated. Ask students to label the stick figure with different things that happen to various areas of their bodies. Give each student an opportunity to explain their diagram.

Prior to this activity, make a copy of Appendix D and cut out the various scenarios. Place these in a container. One at a time, direct students to pull out one of the scenarios and to read it out loud. Then ask them to rate the anger that they would feel on a scale of 1-10 and to describe how they would calm themselves down.

Explain that counting to ten while taking deep breaths is an impulse control technique that seems to work well for most people. Lead a brief exercise practicing the counting technique and allow students to discuss whether or not they feel that the technique might work for them. Allow the students to brainstorm additional techniques which have been useful to them or may be useful to them in the future. Write each of the techniques on the chalk/dry erase board and survey the students on which have been beneficial or which seem like they could work in the future.

On a dry erase board, write the phrase "It's not fair, he always starts it and I am the one who gets in trouble. I am so angry I just want to punch him." Ask students to identify examples of positive self-talk to calm themselves down in this situation. Write the examples beneath the statement.

How To Use Reproducible Sheets:

Reproducible Worksheet 7.1

On Target with Anger, asks students to prioritize those things which make them angry.

Talk about it. Ask students to present their targets and point out any patterns which they may have become aware of.

Reproducible Worksheet 7.2

When I get Angry..., asks students to consider the subtle cues their minds and bodies send when they are becoming angry.

Talk about it. Ask students to discuss which parts of their body respond the quickest and strongest to angry feelings and which responses are the easiest to see or feel. Discuss any responses not listed on the worksheet.

Reproducible Worksheet 7.3

Explore your Options, asks students to consider impulsive and appropriate actions for anger provoking situations.

Talk about it. Discuss which impulse control techniques would be beneficial in controlling anger.

Reproducible Worksheet 7.4

Weigh it Out, asks students to take a look at the pros and cons for displaying impulsive behaviors when angry.

Talk about it. Ask students the implications of this illustration (what it means to them), and if this helps them to understand the impact that poor impulse control can have in their daily lives.

Reproducible Worksheet 7.5

Remember Your Tool Box, asks students to select helpful anger management techniques to defuse anger. Students are given a list of possible anger evoking situations and asked to "pull a tool" from the anger management tool box.

Talk about it. Ask students which "tool" they find most helpful and why. Explain that each tool may not be appropriate in each situation and that they must practice these tools to get good at using them.

On Target with Anger

Recognizing situations where anger arises is an important part of being able to control angry impulses. Write down things that make you angry on the target below, with the thing that makes you feel the angriest in the bull's eye and the things that make you the least angry in the outer most circle.

When I Get Angry...

Recognizing changes in your body can help you to get a head start on your anger management. Complete each sentence about how different parts of your body respond to anger.

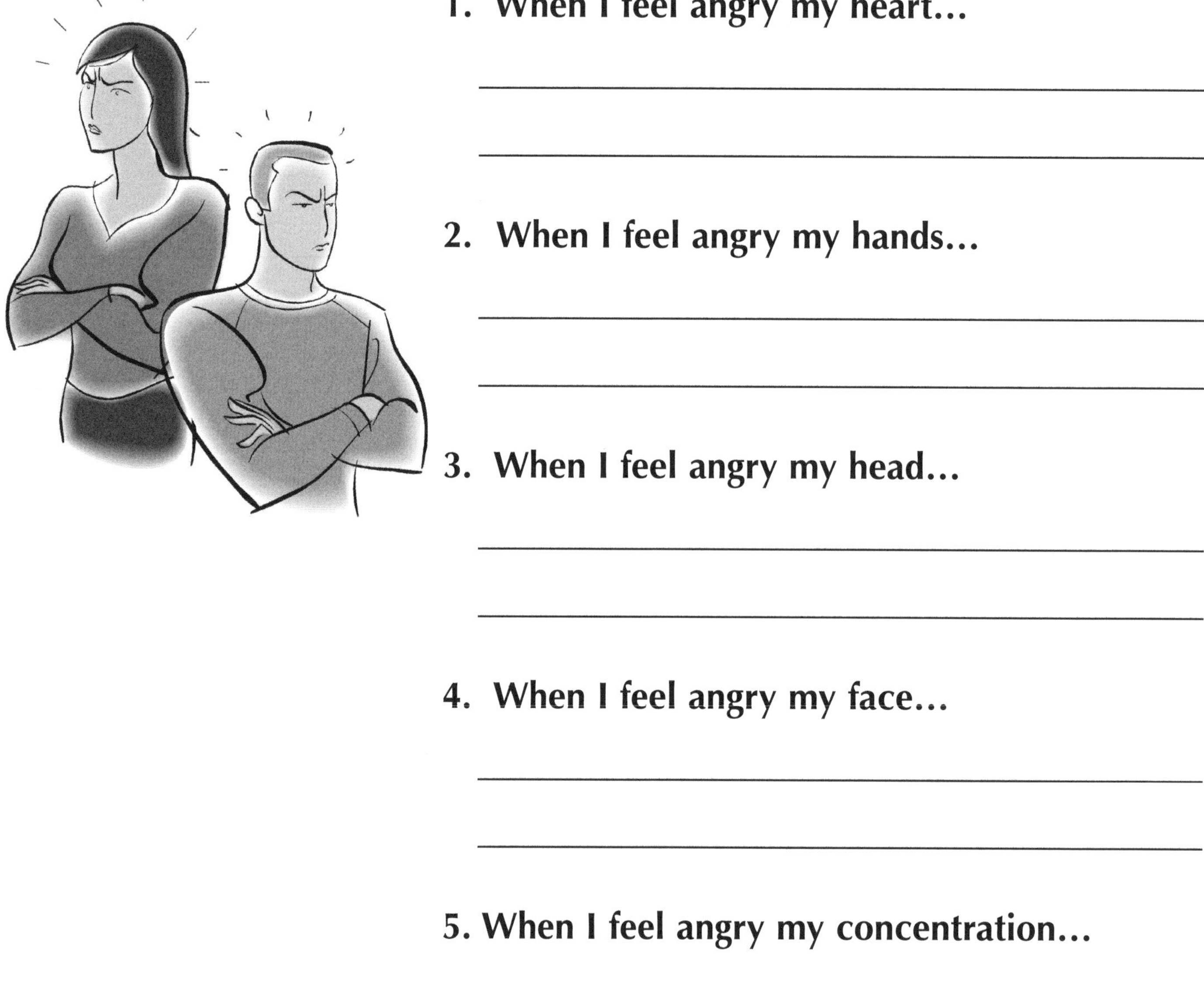

1. When I feel angry my heart...

____

____

2. When I feel angry my hands...

____

____

3. When I feel angry my head...

____

____

4. When I feel angry my face...

____

____

5. When I feel angry my concentration...

____

____

6. When I feel angry my stomach...

____

____

Seeing the difference between impulsive and appropriate behaviors can inspire you to make good choices. For each scenario below, write down one impulsive (inappropriate) course of action and one appropriate course of action.

1. Someone removes your hat from your head and refuses to return it.

Impulsive –

____

____

Appropriate –

____

____

2. You are in the middle of hanging out with friends. Your parent arrives to tell you that you must come home, immediately, to do chores. You are embarrassed by this and don't want to go home.

Impulsive –

____

____

Appropriate –

____

____

3. You forget to bring your math homework to school for the 3rd time. Your teacher informs you that you must go to detention in order to complete your work.

Impulsive –

____

____

Appropriate –

____

____

After answering the question below, use the lines on the scale to write down positive and negative consequences to your response. Pretend that each consequence weighs 10 lbs. When your lists are complete add up the total weight on each side and share your results.

What is an impulse that you act on when feeling angry?

____

____

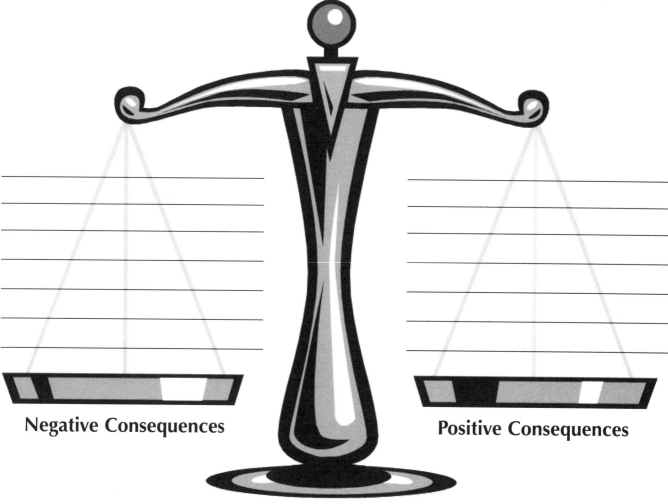

Negative Consequences

Positive Consequences

Total = ________ lbs.

Total = ________ lbs.

Remember Your Tool Box

Using anger management techniques to help diffuse your anger can improve your ability to control your impulses. Draw a line from each situation on the left to an anger management "tool" on the right which you would use. There is more than one "tool" which could work in each situation, so just pick the one that is right for you.

You have been waiting in a long line at the convenience store to buy a drink. When it is almost your turn someone cuts in line.

Your parents ground you for something that was not your fault. When you try to explain, they say that they, "Don't want to hear it!"

Your younger siblings are annoying you during your favorite television program. You ask them to stop but they keep getting louder.

While eating lunch in the cafeteria, someone across the table spills catsup on your new shirt.

As you are walking through the hall between classes, someone trips you and laughs with his friends as you stumble.

Lesson 8

EMPATHY: How can I WALK in someone else's SHOES without getting ATHLETE'S FOOT?

OBJECTIVE:

At the end of this lesson students will be able to

- Recognize the importance of empathy
- Define and describe the concept of empathy
- Better read others' facial expressions, body language and voice tone
- Identify appropriate empathic responses

MATERIALS NEEDED:

Paper, old magazines and newspapers, scissors, glue, video or DVD, video or DVD player, pencils, markers, construction paper, and an article regarding a tragic event.

SCRIPT:

Empathy is the ability to identify with another person's situation or feelings. It means that you are so aware of the other person's emotions that you can feel a bit of that same feeling yourself. You are truly able to "walk in someone else's shoes." One of the amazing parts about empathy, is that you are able to do this without the other person even having to say a word. You just "get it" by reading their facial expressions, watching their body language and listening to their word choices and voice tones.

Empathy also involves letting this shared feeling motivate you to do something positive. You may say something or act in a particular manner that lets the other person know that you understand how they feel. The three (3) steps of empathy which we will be learning more about include:

- Recognize or "read" the other person's feeling
- Allow yourself to share in those feelings
- Give a supportive response (say or do something that lets the other person know you share their feeling)

RATIONALE:

There is evidence that impulsive youth exhibit less empathy than other children (Miller, 1989; Smith, 1998; Wied, Goudena & Matthys, 2005). This may be based on deficits in the ability to read others' feelings because of difficulties with *stopping* and *thinking*. Empathy development is critical for healthy functioning in multiple domains. Indeed, strong empathy has been associated with self-esteem (Griffin-Shirley, & Nes, 2005), academic performance (Liff, 2003), forgiveness in relationships (Paleari, Regalia, & Fincham, 2005) and the development of prosocial behaviors (e.g. Denham & Burger, 1991; Eisenberg, McCreath, & Ahn, 1988; Staub, 1995). Both empathy and role-taking have been associated with imaginative thinking, a characteristic needed for creativity and humor (Strayer & Roberts, 1989).

DISCUSSION QUESTIONS:

- Can you think of a time when you shared someone else's feelings (i.e. shared someone else's joy or shared someone else's pain)? What was that experience like for each of you?
- Why do you think that empathy is important? What would the world be like if no one felt empathy?
- What does a person's face, body and voice look and sound like when they are angry? Happy? Sad? Scared?
- What kinds of things could you say to someone who is feeling sad? What kinds of things could you say to someone who is feeling excited?
- What do you think it means to "walk in someone else's shoes?"

ACTIVITIES:

1

Play Feelings Charades. Have students take turns showing particular emotions on their faces while the other students guess what feeling it is. Another version of Feelings Charades is to cover up the student's face with a large piece of paper and have her/him show a feeling with her/his body while the other students guess what feeling it is.

Instruct the students to create a Feelings Collage. Have them cut out pictures of people from old magazines or newspapers and glue them to a poster board. Then have them write down the feeling words under the pictures.

Tape a movie or TV show segment (not a cartoon) prior to meeting with the students. Preferably choose something that the students have not seen before. Then show the tape with the sound turned off. Ask the students to think about the thoughts and feelings of the characters. Pause the tape from time to time and ask the students what they think is going on.

Ask students to break up into pairs. Instruct them to sit facing one another with their knees one inch apart (in other words, as close as possible without touching). Have one member of the pair slowly make various feelings faces. Have the other person "mirror" those facial expressions – copying the exact look of the other's head, eyes, mouth, etc. Have the students trade roles so that each student gets to mirror the other.

Give each student a piece of paper and a pencil. Invite one of the students to the front of the room to stand. Explain that the rest of the students are to think about this student. Then explain that you will be reading a question with four (4) possible answers (a, b, c, and d) and that the group is to think about how the student who is standing (not themselves) would respond. They then try to guess the standing student's response by writing down a, b, c, or d, depending on which answer they think applies to the person who is standing.

After everyone has written down the letter of their response choice, ask the standing student what the correct answer is. See how many correct responses there are. Repeat this until everyone has had several chances to be the one in the front of the class. Potential questions are limitless with this activity. Some examples are:

QUESTION: What makes you feel most angry?
CHOICES:
a) When someone starts a rumor about you
b) When your teacher blames you for something you didn't do
c) When your brother or sister uses your stuff without asking
d) When someone "steals" your girl/boyfriend

QUESTION: What makes you feel most embarrassed?
CHOICES:
a) Forgetting to zip your zipper
b) Falling in the hallway
c) Walking into the bathroom of the opposite sex
d) Sneezing all over someone

ACTIVITIES:

QUESTION: What makes you feel happiest?
CHOICES:
a) Friends
b) Good grades
c) Music
d) Having a girl/boyfriend

QUESTION: What makes you feel proudest?
CHOICES:
a) Winning in sports
b) Making a good grade
c) Doing a good job with your chores
d) Controlling your temper

QUESTION: If you could have one wish come true, what would it be?
CHOICES:
a) To be even more attractive
b) To be better at sports
c) To be more popular
d) To be really smart

QUESTION: If you were stranded on an island for a week what one thing would you take with you?
CHOICES:
a) A Bible
b) A basketball
c) A comic book
d) A toothbrush

QUESTION: How would you feel if a group of kids wouldn't let you sit with them at lunch?
CHOICES:
a) Angry
b) Sad
c) Disappointed
d) Embarrassed

QUESTION: How would you feel if someone offered to give you drugs?
CHOICES:
a) Angry
b) Scared
c) Confused
d) Embarrassed

Distribute construction paper and markers. Direct the students to think of a friend who is either celebrating something (i.e. a birthday, an accomplishment, a rite of passage, etc.) or is having a difficult time with something (i.e. a death, a divorce, a poor grade, etc.). Encourage students to make and decorate a card for this friend. If assistance is needed for what to write, encourage students to help one another.

Find an article in the newspaper or internet of a tragic event that has happened recently and make copies for all of the students. Ask the group to break up into smaller groups of 3-4 students in order to come up with a way that they can help. Examples include writing letters to the victim's family, writing letters to their state legislator advocating for new policies, creating a support group that deals with such tragedies, etc. Then ask the groups to follow through with their ideas.

How To Use Reproducible Sheets:

Reproducible Worksheet 8.1

Reading Others Feelings, allows students to examine the facial expressions of seven (7) children and to match a feelings word to the face.

Talk about it. Ask students to specifically describe the facial expressions that let them know a particular feeling (i.e. descriptions of brows, eyes, mouth, etc.)

Reproducible Worksheet 8.2

Identifying Others' Feelings, presents students with several scenarios where they must stop and think about the situation and identify a feeling that the person in the scenario might be feeling. A list of feeling words is provided but students need not be limited to these words.

Talk about it. Ask students how they were able to figure out what the characters were feeling. Discuss what appropriate responses would be for each scenario.

Reproducible Worksheet 8.3

Imagine, asks students to imagine the feelings of a custodian, principal, secretary and teacher. Then they are asked to name events that might cause these people to feel happy, sad, surprised, angry, embarrassed and confused.

Talk about it. Sometimes young people don't realize that adults have feelings too. Discuss this idea and then ask students what they can take away (or do differently) from doing this worksheet.

Reproducible Worksheet 8.4

Rating My Empathic Behaviors, asks students to examine a list of empathic behaviors and to think about the frequency with which they practice these. They are then to rank them 1-10 in the order with which they actually do them.

Talk about it. Ask students to list other kinds of empathic behaviors or Random Acts of Kindness.

Reproducible Worksheet 8.5

Choosing Empathic Statements, asks students to consider particular scenarios and, using a multiple choice format, to select the best empathic response to each situation.

Talk about it. Discuss the impact of words. Ask students how words can help or hurt.

Reproducible Worksheet 8.6

Lending a Helping Hand, invites students to recognize times when they have been helpful and to identify the feelings associated with these helpful behaviors. They are then asked to internalize these feelings and to identify themselves as empathic people.

Talk about it. Discuss the kinds of feelings that helping others produces. Ask students if they would like to share with the group some of the helping behaviors they listed on their worksheets.

Reading Others' Feelings

Stop and *think* about what feelings look like on others. Draw a line from the feeling words on the left to the feeling faces on the right.

EMBARRASSED

CONFUSED

NERVOUS

BORED

PROUD

HAPPY

FURIOUS

EXCITED

SAD

Stop and *think* how others might feel in the following situations. Using the words listed below (or any that you can think of) write in one or two feelings for each situation.

HAPPY	SAD	ANGRY	SCARED
PROUD	SILLY	HURT	FRUSTRATED
NERVOUS	LONELY	WORRIED	EMBARRASSED

1. Marco dropped his lunch tray all over himself. Everyone who saw it happen laughed hysterically. How might Marco feel?

2. Jermaine has been living with his grandparents since he was a baby. He just found out that his grandfather was diagnosed with congestive heart failure. How might Jermaine feel?

3. Maria made straight As for the first time in her life after working really hard all semester. How might Maria feel?

4. Keiko works really hard in math but never seems to make very good grades on her homework or on her tests. How might Keiko feel?

5. Naomi just found out that she was elected class president. How might Naomi feel?

IMAGINE

IMAGINE WHAT IT WOULD BE LIKE IF YOU . . .

1. **. . . were a custodian**

   What would make you happy?____________________

   What would make you sad? ____________________

   What would embarrass you? ____________________

2. **. . . were a principal?**

   What would make you happy?____________________

   What would make you sad? ____________________

   What would embarrass you? ____________________

3. **. . . were a school secretary?**

   What would make you happy?____________________

   What would make you sad? ____________________

   What would embarrass you? ____________________

4. **. . . were a teacher?**

   What would make you happy?____________________

   What would make you sad? ____________________

   What would embarrass you? ____________________

Rating My Empathic Behaviors

Rate yourself on the following empathic behaviors by dividing them into the three (3) categories of Best, Good, and Could Use Some Work. List three (3) empathy skills in each category.

	Best	Good	Could Use Some Work
I ask people about their feelings.	❑	❑	❑
I congratulate others on their successes.	❑	❑	❑
I show in an interest in what others' have to say.	❑	❑	❑
I can tell what other people are feeling by the look on their faces.	❑	❑	❑
I like to hear others' point of view.	❑	❑	❑
I like to do nice things for others.	❑	❑	❑
I can "put myself in someone else's shoes."	❑	❑	❑
I am concerned when others feel sad or worried.	❑	❑	❑
I can tell what other people are feeling by the tone of their voices.	❑	❑	❑

Best:

____

Good:

____

Could Use Some Work:

____

CHOOSING  STATEMENTS

DIRECTIONS: Read each of the following situations and the responses that are listed under them. Circle the response that best shows empathy.

1. **Your friend's mother is in the hospital with a serious illness and your friend is quite worried about her.**
   a. You ask your friend if s/he would like you to go with her/him to visit her/his mother in the hospital.
   b. You ask your friend what s/he is doing this weekend.
   c. You tell your friend a joke to distract her/him.
   d. You tell your friend that it is silly to be so worried.

2. **Your best friend is really excited because s/he just got a really cool computer game. It was a game that you really wanted.**
   a. You accuse her/him of bragging.
   b. You change the subject and won't talk about it.
   c. You go home and beg your parent to buy you one.
   d. You say, "That's great!"

3. **Someone on your soccer team missed making a goal at the end of the championship game and caused the team to lose. S/he looks really sad and embarrassed.**
   a. You complain to your teammates about how bad a player s/he is.
   b. You say to her/him, "Tough break. Don't feel bad. You played well overall. It could have happened to any of us."
   c. You don't say anything.
   d. You go up to her/him and say, "You stink!"

4. **Your friend is getting ready to make a speech at an assembly and s/he is pretty nervous.**
   a. You go hang out with another friend who is in a better mood.
   b. You say, "Stop being so nervous!"
   c. You tell her/him you understand how s/he feels because you were really nervous, too, before you gave a speech in class last year.
   d. You tell her/him to "Chill out."

5. **Your friend gets teased for being short and s/he really hates it.**
   a. You tell her/him that it's no big deal.
   b. You ask the other kids to quit teasing her/him.
   c. You change the subject when s/he tries to talk about it.
   d. You join in the teasing to look cool.

LENDING A HELPING HAND

There are many ways that people show empathy by helping. Think about ways in which someone might need help. List as many as you can think of.

#1. ______________________________

#2. ______________________________

#3. ______________________________

#4. ______________________________

#5. ______________________________

#6. ______________________________

#7. ______________________________

#8. ______________________________

#9. ______________________________

#10. ______________________________

Have you ever helped in any of the ways that you listed above?

YES **NO**

Which ones have you done?

____

____

Lesson 9

Social Skills: Keeping it Friendly

Objective:

At the end of this lesson students will be able to

- Identify the behaviors that make good social skills
- Recognize that making others feel special is important to being liked
- Discuss ways in which to select trustworthy friends

Materials Needed:

Paper, pens/pencils, dry erase board or chalkboard with markers or chalk

Script:

Having friends is a wonderful part of life. It's great to have friends to hang out with, to share problems with, to celebrate successes with, and to stick up for you. But to have a friend you must be a friend. That means that you must act in ways that take the other person into account and make the other person feel special. If you can make someone feel special s/he will want to be your friend.

It is also important to choose your friends wisely. Although you should treat all people with respect, not everyone needs to be a close friend. Most people choose friends who like to do some of the same kinds of things they do. But it is also important to choose friends who are loyal to you and who are not a bad influence.

Rationale:

Attaining social skills for interacting successfully with peers is an important achievement in childhood. Having poor social skills in childhood is a predictor of poor psychosocial adjustment in life (Asher, & Coie, 1990). Impulsive youth often suffer peer rejection and have more problems in their social relationships than do other teens (Corapci, 2008; Landau & Moore, 1991; Olson, 1989; Patterson & Newman, 1993). Indeed, research shows that individuals who are impulsive have poorer social problem-solving skills and poorer social cooperativeness (McMurran, Blair, & Egan, 2002; Olson, 1989). Their propensity to change activities and topics of conversation too quickly often results in poorly coordinated interactions. They also have difficulty taking time to get to know others' interests, or may be unable to read social cues in order to respond appropriately. Despite these problems, however, research suggests that intervention can assist impulsive young people in improving their social skills (e.g. McMahon & Washburn, 2003).

Discussion Questions:

- Why is it important to have friends? What are friends good for?
- What are ways you can make friends? What are ways you can keep friends after you make them?
- What are behaviors that might cause you to lose friends?
- How do you choose friends? What kind of friend do you look for?

ACTIVITIES:

1

Have two (2) students volunteer to play "Talk Show Host." Most young people are familiar with television programs where a host interviews a guest. Have one of the students play the "host" and the other play the "guest." Direct the "host" to show an interest in the guest by asking interview questions. Encourage the host to think about the life of the "guest" and to ask specific questions based on the guest's hobbies and activities. Encourage the "host" to ask mostly "What" and "How" questions rather than "Why" questions. This exercise teaches students how to show an interest in others.

Ask the students to sit in a circle. Instruct them to think about the person sitting on their right. Then go around and have each student give a compliment to the person on their right. The person receiving the compliment should then say, "Thank you." When everyone has both given and received a compliment discuss how it felt to receive a compliment. Discuss how making others feel special helps in making and keeping friends.

Direct students to break up into small groups of 3-4 people. Ask each group to brainstorm a list of qualities that they look for in a friend. Have someone in the group write these down on a piece of paper. When the list is complete, ask the groups to cooperatively agree on the three (3) most important qualities. Discuss what social skills were needed to complete this task.

On a dry erase or chalkboard write down the following famous quotations about friendship. Ask students to discuss their meanings and how applicable they might be to their own friendships:

"Be slow to fall into friendship; but when thou art in, continue firm and constant."

— *Socrates*

"Anybody can sympathize with the sufferings of a friend, but it requires a very fine nature to sympathize with a friend's success."

— *Oscar Wilde*

"I will speak ill of no man, and speak all the good I know of everybody."

— *Benjamin Franklin*

"What is a friend? A single soul in two bodies."

— *Aristotle*

"In the end, we will remember not the words of our enemies, but the silence of our friends."

— *Martin Luther King Jr.*

Divide students into 3 groups, labeling each group as a particular setting where manners are used (i.e. school, home, and community). Ask each group to think about the manners that are expected in their setting. Discuss the similarities and differences between settings.

HOW TO USE REPRODUCIBLE SHEETS:

Reproducible Worksheet 9.1

Making Others Feel Important, asks students to think about four (4) of their friends and the things that they can do to make each particular friend feel important. Encourage students to differentiate each friend and not simply write one generic response for all of the friends.

Talk about it. Ask students why it is important to make other people feel important. Discuss the behaviors that make almost everyone feel important and what behaviors might be unique to the individual.

Reproducible Worksheet 9.2

Social Skills Evaluation, has students evaluating themselves on important social skills. They are asked to rate themselves with 1-5 stars on the behaviors of sharing, saying "Hi," smiling at others, inviting others to play, letting others go first, letting others decide what to play, keeping friends' secrets and sticking up for friends.

Talk about it. Ask students to discuss their strengths and weaknesses. Discuss ways in which students can strengthen their weaknesses.

Reproducible Worksheet 9.3

What does it mean? Reading Social Cues, asks students to read various scenarios where there are physical cues to peers' reactions. They are asked to interpret the meanings of the cues and to describe an appropriate way to respond.

Talk about it. Discuss ways that people communicate through body language.

Reproducible Worksheet 9.4

Evaluating a Friendship, asks students to keep a particular current friendship in mind while rating the quality of that friendship on several dimensions (e.g. listening, inviting, sticking up for, etc.). A total score is obtained and compared against a description of the quality of the relationship.

Talk about it. Discuss students' feelings about the scores that they obtained on this worksheet. Discuss how one might give up a friendship if it was not a healthy one.

Reproducible Worksheet 9.5

Listening to Body Language, asks students to identify the body language associated with appropriate active listening. They are asked to label the appropriate actions for different body parts when they are listening to someone.

Talk about it. Discuss the benefits of using good active listening skills. Discuss speakers' perceptions of people who do not use good active listening skills.

Reproducible Worksheet 9.6

Build-a-Friend, asks students to examine various qualities that they might find in a friend and to circle the three (3) qualities that they value *most* in a friend and to put an X through three (3) of the qualities that they least value in a friend.

Talk about it. Discuss students' choices. Then discuss if it is important to have the same qualities in oneself that one looks for in a friend.

Making Others Feel Important

Dale Carnegie, the author of the massive bestseller, *How to Win Friends and Influence People*, said that one of the six ways to make others like you is to "Make the other person feel important and do it sincerely." This is still incredibly true today. Some of the things that we do to make others feel important are compliment them, let them go first, listen to them, invite them over, let them choose what to do, etc. Every person has different things that make her/him feel important. Think of four (4) friends or classmates. What makes them feel important? Write their names and the things that you can do to make them feel valuable or important.

(1) MY FRIEND,

______________________________,

FEELS IMPORTANT WHEN I

______________________________.

(2) MY FRIEND,

______________________________,

FEELS IMPORTANT WHEN I

______________________________.

(3) MY FRIEND,

______________________________,

FEELS IMPORTANT WHEN I

______________________________.

(4) MY FRIEND,

______________________________,

FEELS IMPORTANT WHEN I

______________________________.

Social Skills Evaluation

Social skills are the behaviors that help us make and keep friends. They are the actions that motivate others to like us. Read the following social skills and rate yourself with stars.

SOCIAL SKILL:		YOUR RATING:
(1)	Smiling at others and saying "Hi" even if I don't know the person well	☆☆☆☆☆
(2)	Being a good listener and showing an interest in others' activities and opinions	☆☆☆☆☆
(3)	Reading other people's body language during conversations so I know when to change the topic or stay on the topic a bit longer	☆☆☆☆☆
(4)	Inviting others to join me when I see that they are alone or left out	☆☆☆☆☆
(5)	Being assertive about my needs while also considering the feelings and needs of others	☆☆☆☆☆
(6)	Resolving conflicts and negotiating win-win solutions when others and I disagree	☆☆☆☆☆
(7)	Keeping friends' secrets even when I am angry with them or know it could make me more popular with others for telling	☆☆☆☆☆
(8)	Sticking up for friends when others speak badly of them	☆☆☆☆☆

WHAT DOES IT MEAN?

READING SOCIAL CUES

It's important to read social cues in order to know how to act or respond. Read the following situations and then write down what you think it means and what you should do about it.

You are standing in a group of peers. You say something that you think is pretty funny. No one laughs and one person rolls her/his eyes.

What does it mean?

____

____

What should you do?

____

____

You are describing a new video game to one of your friends. As you really get into describing it, your friend starts to look away every now and then.

What does it mean?

____

____

What should you do?

____

____

You are talking with a classmate. You are really excited but you notice that the classmate keeps leaning back away from you.

What does it mean?

____

____

What should you do?

____

____

EVALUATING A FRIENDSHIP

Think about a particular friend that you currently have. Do not say the name of the person out loud or write it down, but keep the person in your mind as you rate her/him 1-5 on the questions below. Circle the number that best describes the frequency in which your friend engages in the behavior described.

1 = Never **2** = Rarely **3** = Sometimes **4** = Frequently **5** = All the time

1. My friend is my friend no matter who is around.	1	2	3	4	5
2. My friend listens to my point of view.	1	2	3	4	5
3. My friend is considerate of my feelings even when we disagree.	1	2	3	4	5
4. My friend calls me and invites me over as much as I call and invite her/him.	1	2	3	4	5
5. My friend never asks me to do anything that I am uncomfortable about.	1	2	3	4	5
6. My friend never asks me to do anything that could get me into trouble.	1	2	3	4	5
7. My friend sticks up for me when others are bugging me.	1	2	3	4	5

Add up the numbers that you have circled. Total: ____________

Examine the level in which this friend is a true friend:

1 – 14: ....Not a friend at all
15 – 21: ....Fair-weathered friend
22 – 28: ....More of an acquaintance
29 – 35: ....Loyal friend

LISTENING TO BODY LANGUAGE

Label the different body parts with the appropriate action to show that you are listening to someone when they talk.

How should each body part respond when you are really paying attention to someone?

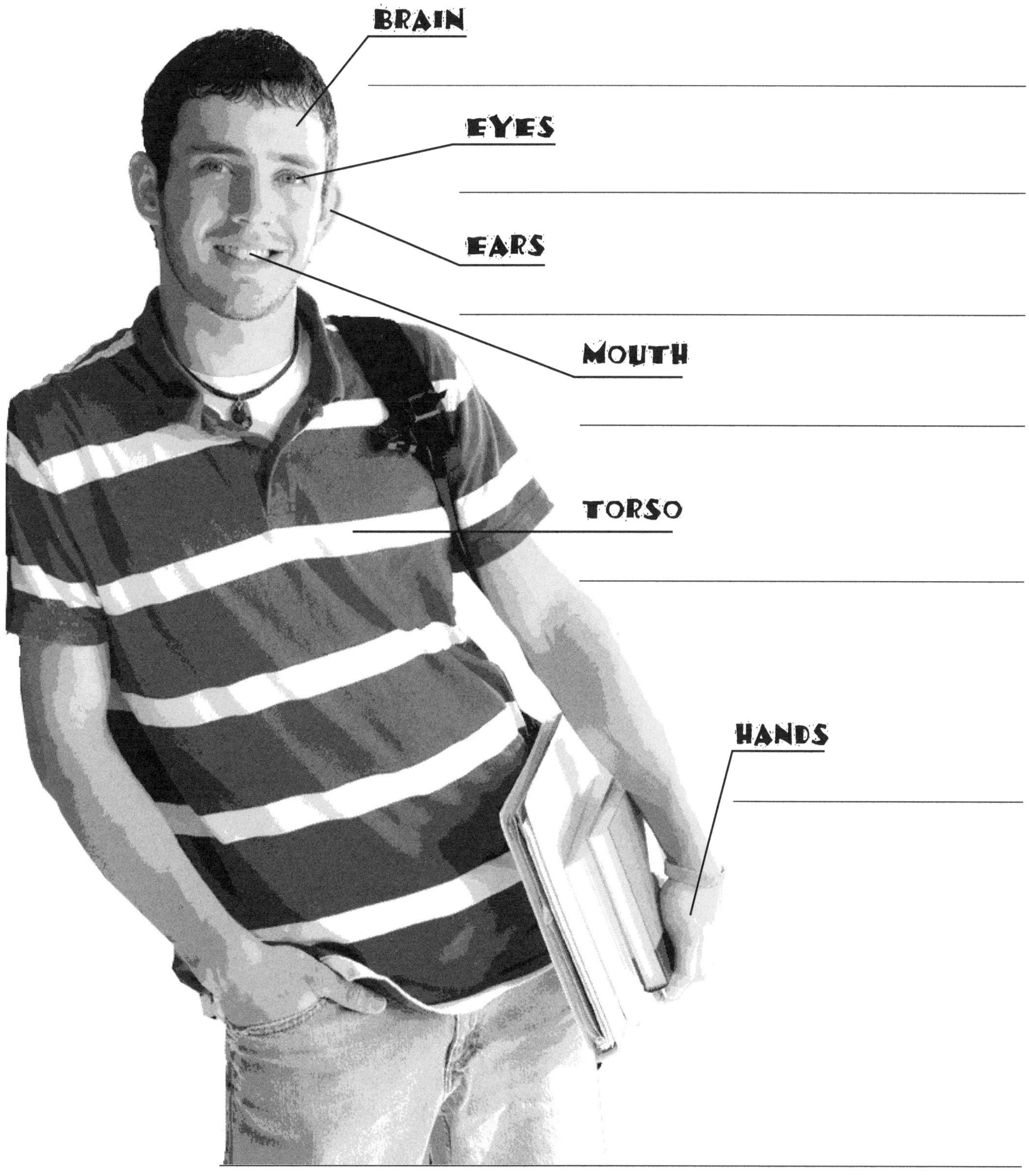

Build-A-Friend

Examine the qualities of a friend listed below. Circle the three (3) qualities that you value *most* in a friend. Then put an X through three (3) of the qualities that you *least* value in a friend. (This might be a good quality but it is not necessarily one that you look for in a friend.)

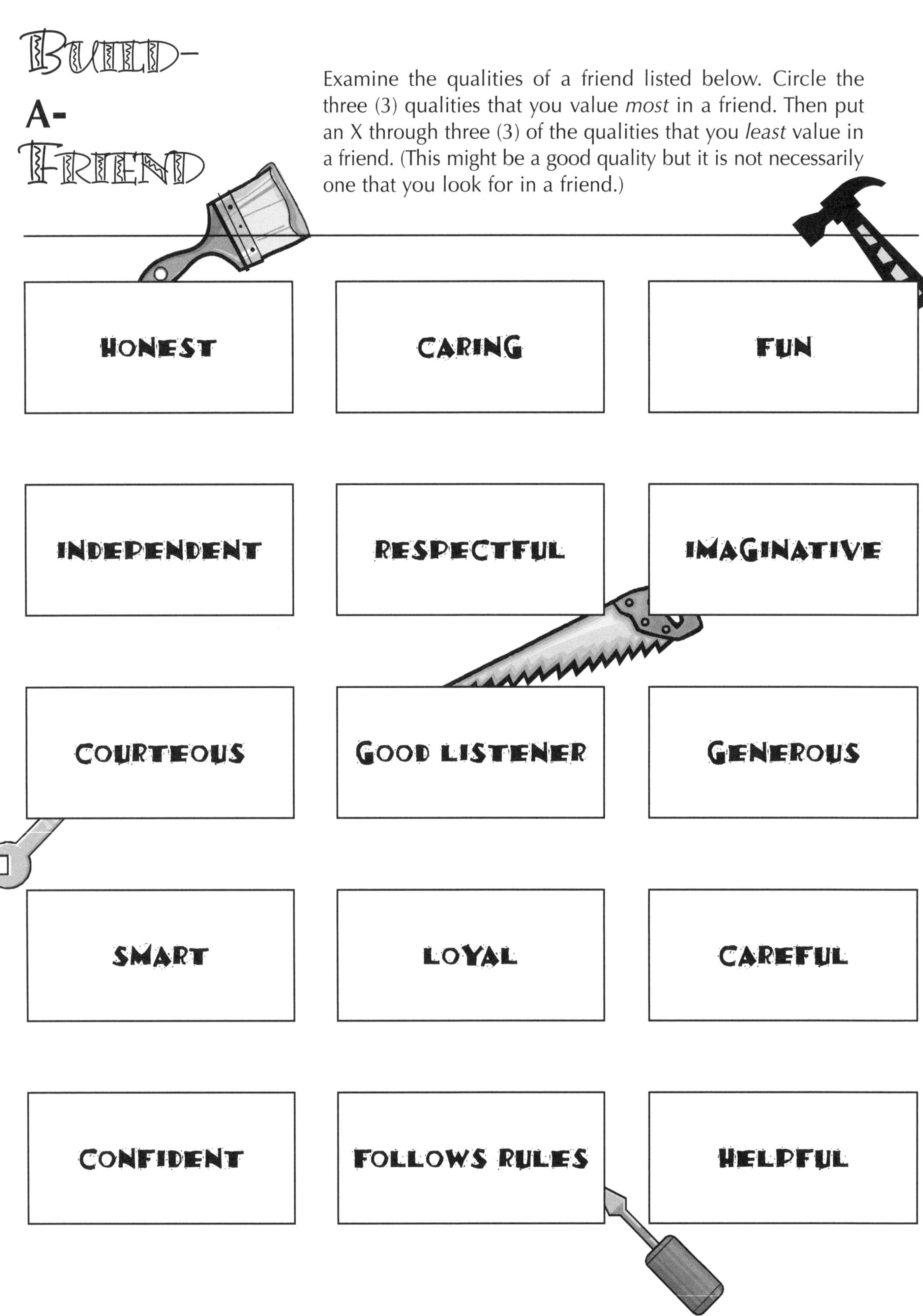

HONEST
CARING
FUN
INDEPENDENT
RESPECTFUL
IMAGINATIVE
COURTEOUS
GOOD LISTENER
GENEROUS
SMART
LOYAL
CAREFUL
CONFIDENT
FOLLOWS RULES
HELPFUL

Boundaries: Living & Coloring within the Lines

Lesson 10

Objective:

At the end of this lesson students will be able to

- Define and describe the purpose of boundaries
- Understand the importance of creating and respecting boundaries
- Recognize social boundaries
- Recognize personal space boundaries

Materials Needed:

Picture of solar system, masking tape, a stick or ruler, decorative items (such as feathers, beads, pieces of leather, etc.), and glue

Script:

A boundary is the edge of something; a line or border that divides things. In sports there is often a boundary. A game is played inside of a boundary and, if a person or a ball goes outside of that boundary, it is called "out of bounds" and it is considered some kind of violation. Boundaries help us to organize and understand the game.

There are other kinds of boundaries in life besides those in games. For example, there are physical space boundaries. If someone stays outside of our personal space boundary we feel comfortable, but if someone steps inside this boundary without our permission we feel uncomfortable. There are also boundaries in conversations (i.e. not interrupting, not talking about certain subjects at certain times, etc.) and boundaries in our various roles (i.e. parents not dumping financial worries onto kids, teachers not acting like students, etc.) Rules are also boundaries. They let us know what is acceptable and unacceptable within our culture.

Boundaries are meant to protect us and keep order in chaos. Learning how to have good boundaries will require you to stop and think about where the boundaries are and how best to respect them.

Rationale:

A boundary is a broad term for where there is some kind of line or border – the place where one thing stops and another begins. While there are physical boundaries such as fences, borders and street lines, there are also invisible boundaries. Most of us recognize that a personal space boundary exists about 30 inches around one's body, although it is not visible to the eye. Other invisible boundaries include rules and laws. There are also boundaries regarding verbal exchanges, roles, and accepting "No." Although boundaries are difficult to define and research, relationship boundary violations are well recognized as a significant factor in the development of psychopathology (e.g. Cicchetti & Howes, 1991; Kerig, 2005).

Impulsive youth tend to overstep more boundaries than other young people. This is due to (1) a poor ability to clearly identify boundaries and/or (2) an impulsive indifference for recognized boundaries. It is therefore helpful to teach impulsive students where boundaries exist and to assist them in recognizing the advantages of respecting boundaries and the consequences for overstepping boundaries (i.e. stop and think!).

Discussion Questions:

- What kinds of games have boundaries? What does it mean if something goes out of the boundaries? Why do you think that some games have boundaries? What would those games be like if they *didn't* have boundaries?
- What are other kinds of tangible boundaries (i.e. borders, fences, walls, doors, etc.)? What are some *in*tangible boundaries (i.e. personal space, rules, roles in relationships, etc.)?
- What kinds of impulses give us trouble respecting boundaries (i.e. the impulse to interrupt, the impulse to go into another person's area without permission, etc.)?
- What happens when someone steps over a boundary without permission?

Activities:

1

Obtain a picture of the solar system (which depicts the paths in which the planets orbit the sun) and display it for the students. Describe how each planet stays on a course (i.e. within particular boundaries). Ask students what would happen if planets moved outside of their boundaries. Emphasize how this is also true of people (i.e. just like planets, if we do not respect boundaries we are not safe, not on course and not functioning properly). Discuss how impulses can tempt us to ignore or forget about boundaries.

Explain to students that rules are boundaries; they divide acceptable from unacceptable behavior. The purpose of rules is to (1) keep us safe, (2) help us to get along with others, and (3) make things as fair as possible. Write these three (3) purposes on a dry erase board or chalkboard. Then explain to the students that you will be reading several rules. As you read them one by one, instruct students to call out which of the three (3) purposes each particular rule serves. (Feel free to add additional rules.)

- Do not drive over the speed limit
- Look both ways before crossing the street
- Do not take merchandise without paying for it
- Do not hit/assault people
- Raise your hand when you know the answer
- Take turns using the computer
- Stand in line when waiting to pay for groceries
- Do not enter others' property without their permission
- Don't lean back in your chair
- Don't talk when the teacher is talking

Discuss how impulse control can help us follow rules.

Using masking tape, create a circle on the floor that is approximately 5-6 feet in diameter. Invite one student at a time to stand in the middle of the circle while other students mill around outside of the circle. Ask the student inside of the circle if s/he feels that people are too close. Then ask one of the students to step inside the circle with the person already in the circle. Now ask both of the students inside the circle if they feel like the other person is too close. Discuss personal space boundaries. Ask students what they should stop and think about in order to respect personal space boundaries.

Using a stick or ruler and decorative items such as feathers, old jewelry, netting, leather strips, stickers, etc., ask students to create a "Talking Stick" that represents their group. Then direct the group to sit in a circle and discuss a lively topic (i.e. something controversial or the planning of an activity for the group), making sure that no one interrupts another by only speaking when they have the Talking Stick in their hand. Explain how the impulse to interrupt crosses a talking boundary. Discuss the experience of taking turns with the Talking Stick.

Place a piece of masking tape down the middle of the room. Explain to students that one side of the tape represents OK and the other side represents NOT OK. Explain that you will be reading off some situations where there is a person, a setting and a topic of conversation. Students are to decide if the topic is OK or NOT OK for the person or setting by placing themselves on the OK or NOT OK side of the tape. Some of the situations are vague and students may be in disagreement about whether it is OK or NOT OK to talk about the topic. Encourage discussion around these situations. Feel free to create some of your own scenarios. Here are a few:

- Talking about homework to your teacher
- Talking about homework to the adult sitting next to you in a bus or airplane
- Talking about homework to a classmate
- Talking about your diarrhea to the doctor
- Talking about your diarrhea to the principal
- Talking about your diarrhea to the girl or guy that you are flirting with
- Talking about all the new clothes you bought to a classmate who is poor
- Talking about all the new clothes you bought to your grandmother
- Talking about all the new clothes you bought to someone sitting behind you in the movie
- Talking about your best friend's crush to another friend
- Talking about your best friend's crush to your best friend's mother
- Talking about your best friend's crush to the person who s/he has the crush on
- Talking about the movie you saw last night during a math test
- Talking about the movie you saw last night at lunch
- Talking about the movie you saw last night in the library

Ask students how they determine if a conversation is appropriate or not (i.e. *stop* and *think*!)

Give students the definition of assuming. Explain that assuming is a boundary intrusion because no one can really go into another person's mind and know what they think. Give each student seven (7) tissues to use as "penalty flags" and instruct them to throw one tissue on the ground each time that you read an example of assuming. Use the following scenarios but feel free to create some of your own (just remember to give students additional tissues!).

- "I didn't do very well on the algebra test. The teacher must think that I am stupid."
- "She had a funny expression on her face just now when she looked at me. She must be mad at me."
- "I can't catch a ball very well. I wonder if any other kids have the same problem."
- "My mom is being awfully quiet. Something really bad must have happened."
- "My friend said she can't go to the mall today. I guess she'll tell me why later."
- "My new haircut looks terrible. I bet everyone notices and makes fun of me."
- "I forgot to put my clean clothes away. Mom had to remind me."
- "My girlfriend just smiled at my best friend. I bet they are hooking up behind my back."
- "My stepdad let my brother use his tools. He must like my brother better than me."
- "My friend has been acting weird lately. I think I'll call her and see if she is angry with me."
- "My best friend didn't call me tonight like s/he usually does. I wonder what happened."
- "My boyfriend didn't call me tonight. I guess we're finished."

Reproducible Worksheet 10.1

Boundary Word Search, allows students the opportunity to have fun while finding words that have meanings related to boundaries.

Talk about it. Ask students if they know what all of the words mean. Then discuss how these all represent boundaries of one sort or another.

Reproducible Worksheet 10.2

Invisible Boundaries, encourages students to stop and think about invisible boundaries and where they might be (i.e. between being curious and being nosey, between bragging and telling good news, between nagging and reminding, between assuming and understanding and between feeling frustrated and feeling furious).

Talk about it. Discuss how difficult it is sometimes to determine where an invisible boundary is. Ask students how impulse control can help them better identify invisible boundaries. Discuss why it might be important to respect boundaries.

Reproducible Worksheet 10.3

STOP and GO, asks students to examine several personal space boundary behaviors and to circle STOP if it is a boundary violation (i.e. sitting too close, grabbing, pushing, kicking and overly personal displays of affection) and to circle GO if it shows good boundaries (i.e. giving others more room, waiting to walk through a doorway).

Talk about it. Ask students to look over the items where they have circled STOP. Discuss which ones they have had impulses to do. Encourage students to identify strategies to stop themselves from crossing these boundaries. Discuss how others feel about them when they are able to stop themselves.

Reproducible Worksheet 10.4

Boundary Crossings, asks students to identify situations where boundaries have either been crossed or respected by placing either a line through or parallel to a vertical line (boundary) next to each statement. (Examples: "LaTisha wants to put on some lip gloss so she gets into Tia's purse and uses hers." "Leela's mother is on the telephone so she waits until she is off to ask her if she can spend the night with Ashley.")

Talk about it. Ask students to discuss how they knew if a boundary had been crossed or not. Ask which scenarios showed good impulse control or poor impulse control.

Reproducible Worksheet 10.5

Finding the Rule, reminds students that there are reasons for rules. There are reasons listed for five (5) unnamed rules and students are asked to identify the specific rules that are being referred to (Answers: Don't interrupt; don't look at others' papers; look both ways or only cross on green; don't physically or verbally abuse others; and stand in line)

Talk about it. Discuss how difficult or easy it is to follow rules. Ask students to discuss what makes it easier to follow rules that they don't like.

Word Search

Find the 10 words listed below in the Word Search

EDGE	BORDER	OUTLINE	LINE
STRIPE	BOUNDARY	LIMIT	PERIMETER
RIM	FRAME		

A	I	I	T	Q	S	J	Q	S	C	P	F	I	S	P	R
S	E	P	G	F	Z	D	N	E	P	C	M	V	B	P	O
T	D	T	H	E	N	T	S	B	E	H	R	E	O	A	E
R	S	N	X	G	V	R	B	P	R	T	L	M	U	B	D
H	S	A	G	R	R	R	N	N	I	R	E	C	N	N	R
T	N	E	A	P	P	L	O	M	M	A	M	E	D	S	T
U	R	V	D	N	E	N	I	U	E	E	R	S	A	E	R
Y	N	C	E	P	W	L	S	N	T	F	E	W	R	E	T
R	E	E	E	D	S	R	E	T	E	L	R	T	Y	F	T
M	P	Q	G	A	G	G	S	A	R	E	I	O	M	N	R
S	G	U	E	F	E	E	I	F	D	I	H	N	A	R	R
C	Z	R	E	E	J	J	F	R	I	M	P	N	E	E	N
B	E	R	V	R	K	F	O	A	N	E	S	E	P	S	O
F	O	D	C	R	T	B	W	M	T	E	T	E	X	P	A
S	G	G	S	Q	F	O	I	E	R	L	T	L	Y	L	W
S	E	Y	E	E	N	N	M	R	T	D	C	M	R	G	C

INVISIBLE BOUNDARIES

Not all boundaries can be seen. But that does not mean that they do not exist! *Stop* and *think* about the boundaries that divide the things below and write down where you think the boundaries are.

Where do you draw the line between being curious and being nosey?

____

____

____

Where do you draw the line between bragging and telling good news?

____

____

____

Where do you draw the line between nagging and reminding?

____

____

____

Where do you draw the line between assuming and understanding?

____

____

____

Where do you draw the line between frustrated and furious?

____

____

____

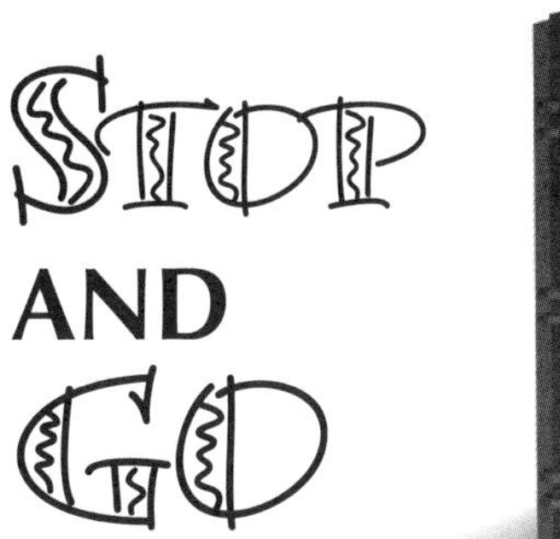

Read the following personal space boundary behaviors. Circle STOP or GO depending on if it is a boundary violation or shows good boundaries.

1. **Carolyn stands right up against James during choir practice even though there is plenty of space on the other side of her.**
   STOP – Boundary Violation **GO** – Good Boundaries
2. **LaVell grabs Josh's backpack off his back.**
   STOP – Boundary Violation **GO** – Good Boundaries
3. **When standing in the lunch line, Semah leaves plenty of space between herself and the person in front to her.**
   STOP – Boundary Violation **GO** – Good Boundaries
4. **Caleb grabs Julie and pushes her into a locker to make a point.**
   STOP – Boundary Violation **GO** – Good Boundaries
5. **Janette swings her legs but makes sure that she keeps from kicking Keiko's seat.**
   STOP – Boundary Violation **GO** – Good Boundaries
6. **Jose holds the door open for Ms. Hanson and waits for her to get all the way through before going through the door himself.**
   STOP – Boundary Violation **GO** – Good Boundaries
7. **Rachel grabs a hat off of Tim's head.**
   STOP – Boundary Violation **GO** – Good Boundaries
8. **Carl pushes others to get in the front of the line.**
   STOP – Boundary Violation **GO** – Good Boundaries
9. **Trey keeps putting his arm around Tiffany even though she has repeatedly asked him to leave her alone.**
   STOP – Boundary Violation **GO** – Good Boundaries
10. **During a group project, Shannon moves her chair a few inches away in order to keep from crowding her group.**
    STOP – Boundary Violation **GO** – Good Boundaries

Boundary

Read the situations below. Put an arrow across the line to the right of each situation if it crosses a boundary and draw a line parallel to the line if it respects a boundary.
Examples:

1. Jaron tells Todd that he doesn't want to play soccer today. Todd keeps asking him over and over and over and over again.

2. Angie is spending the night with Karen. At 3 a.m. Angie wakes up Karen to talk about how sad she is that Hunter broke up with her.

3. Xavier is excited to tell his friends that he is going to Six Flags with his grandparents but he notices that they are playing a video game so he waits until they are finished to tell them.

4. Carmetta wants to comb her hair so she gets into Tonya's purse and uses her brush and mirror without asking.

5. Leslie wants to ask her mother if she can spend the night with Erin, but she notices that her mother is taking a nap so she waits until she wakes up.

6. Kisha and her boyfriend have been arguing a lot lately. At a dinner party that her parents are giving she tells a new friend of her mother's all about it.

7. Miguel is furious with a classmate for embarrassing him in front of a group of guys. He wants to hit him but walks away instead.

FINDING THE RULE

Rules serve multiple purposes. They keep us safe, help us to get along with others, keep things organized, and make things as fair as possible – to name a few. Listed below are reasons for several different rules that you are familiar with. See if you can figure out what the rule is from the reason for the rule.

REASON FOR THE RULE	WHAT IS THE RULE?
To help people say what they need to say when they want to say it.	______________________ ______________________
To help make taking a test fair.	______________________ ______________________
To help people feel safe when they are crossing the street.	______________________ ______________________
To help people feel safe if they disagree with a friend.	______________________ ______________________
To keep everyone organized while buying tickets at a football game.	______________________ ______________________

Lesson 11

Peer Pressure: Staying STRONG When Others Try to PEERsuade ME

OBJECTIVE:

At the end of this lesson students will be able to

- Recognize areas of their lives which are most influenced by peer pressure
- Identify situations where peer pressure has led to impulsive behaviors
- Recognize the benefits of withstanding peer pressure
- Utilize impulse control techniques to help withstand peer pressure
- Say "no" to peer pressure in a variety of situations

MATERIALS NEEDED:

Pens/pencils, paper, a copy of Appendix E, scissors, and a small container

SCRIPT:

Being a part of a social group or wanting to be a part of a social group can place us in a situation where we must make decisions with or against the group. Sometimes what the group approves of is positive and the decision is simple, but sometimes the group may want us to do something that is inappropriate and has negative consequences. Regardless, there is pressure on us to behave according to what the group thinks is right, this is called peer pressure.

Peer pressure can be communicated openly ("Come on, no one is looking; just take it") or peer pressure can be an unspoken rule of the group (in order to be accepted in our group you must wear a certain brand of jeans or use inappropriate language). Though most of us consider it important to "fit in" and be accepted by a group, it is also important that we think for ourselves and take the time to consider the possible consequences for following the crowd.

RATIONALE:

Peer pressure is among the greatest factors influencing the decisions of adolescents on a day-to-day basis. As teens spend less time interacting with parents and more time interacting with peers, peer relationships begin to play a much greater role in determining behavior. Part of normal adolescent development is the desire to "fit in" with peers. However, if the peer group is engaged in unhealthy behaviors, a teen is faced with the dilemma of fitting in or standing up for her/his beliefs. If the teen struggles with impulsivity, s/he may not consider the consequences of following the crowd. Peer influence then results in unhealthy, risky behavior (Mack, Strong & Kowalski, 2007; Morrongiello & Dawber, 2004). Teaching impulsive adolescents to identify various types of peer pressure, to recognize the benefits of thinking for oneself, and to consider the consequences to withstand negative peer pressure can help them stay out of trouble and boost their self-esteem.

DISCUSSION QUESTIONS:

- What are some examples of "open" forms of peer pressure (i.e. "Come on, everyone is doing it," "You better do it, I thought you were cool," etc.) that you have either personally experienced or seen someone experience?
- What are some of the less "open" forms of peer pressure that you have seen (i.e. groups talking a certain way, groups pressuring you to dress a certain way, attitudes towards different things like school, music, parents, etc.)?
- Does peer pressure have to be verbal? If not, what are some other ways that kids put pressure on each other to act in the same ways?
- What are some of the consequences that might occur when someone gives in to peer pressure? When someone gets in trouble for doing something they were pressured to do, do the people who pressured them get in trouble also?
- What are some ways you could withstand the impulses to give in to peer pressure or have seen someone withstand the impulses to give in to peer pressure? How do you think other people would react to you or the person who withstood the peer pressure?

ACTIVITIES:

1

Make a copy of Appendix E. Cut out the scenarios and place them in a container. Ask two (2) student volunteers to come to the front of the room. One of the students will draw a peer pressure scenario and read it to the other student. The other student will then practice a method for refusing the peer pressure example. Following this brief role-play, the student who presented the peer pressure example will sit down with the group and the student who provided the refusal method will choose another volunteer and then draw and read a peer pressure example to the new participant, who then has the opportunity to practice a refusal method. This continues until all of the scenarios have been used.

Explain to students that we all experience some level of peer pressure every day. Review the different kinds of peer pressure with the students (i.e. invitations, taunts, unspoken pressure to follow the norms, peers making negative activities openly available, etc.). Then ask students to identify and discuss some experiences that they have had with peer pressure, and the impulses that accompanied the peer pressure (i.e. the impulse to "give in," the impulse to say "no," etc.). Discuss the styles of peer pressure that students have been exposed to.

Ask students to yell out "yes" or "no" in response to the following situations:

- Your friend is doing poorly in math. S/he is afraid that s/he might fail if s/he can't pass the next test. S/he asks to see your paper during the next test.
- You are afraid of heights and your friend wants you to jump off the bridge into the lake. The other people in the group begin to call you "chicken."
- You love to play tennis and your friend asks you to play tennis after school.
- You have a ton of homework to do before tomorrow. Your friend is begging you to come over and watch a movie.
- You are at a party and someone offers you a drink of their beer, saying "One drink won't hurt."
- Your friend is struggling in English. S/he asks if you will help him/her study for the next test.
- One of your friends says that s/he needs a lot of money fast. S/he asks if you will ask your parents for the money and not tell them who it is for.
- While you are hanging out with your friends after school, one of them offers you a cigarette.

Explain to students that *stopping and thinking* about the consequences of a choice prior to acting is, as we have learned in previous lessons, one of the best ways to control impulses. Ask students to think of a time when they resisted peer pressure and explain the secret to their success.

ACTIVITIES:

Read the following poem to the students and discuss its meaning as it relates to peer pressure.

The Road Not Taken
by Robert Frost

Two roads diverged in a yellow wood,
And sorry I could not travel both
And be one traveler, long I stood
And looked down one as far as I could
To where it bent in the undergrowth.

Then took the other, as just as fair,
And having perhaps the better claim,
Because it was grassy and wanted wear;
Though as for that the passing there
Had worn them really about the same.

And both that morning equally lay
In leaves no step had trodden black.
Oh, I kept the first for another day!
Yet knowing how way leads on to way,
I doubted if I should ever come back.

I shall be telling this with a sigh
Somewhere ages and ages hence:
Two roads diverged in a wood, and I —
I took the one less traveled by,
And that has made all the difference.

How To Use Reproducible Sheets:

Reproducible Worksheet 11.1

Peer Pressure Crossword, asks students to identify various terms associated with peer pressure to use in a crossword puzzle. Words across are clothes, no, impulse, alcohol, and friends. Words going down are taunt, cheat, popular, invite, and norm.

Talk about it. Discuss the various terms and any thoughts that the students might have regarding the pressures that they feel to conform to their peers.

Reproducible Worksheet 11.2

Pump it up!, asks students to rate the level of pressure (i.e. how hard it would be to say "no," etc.) they have experienced or would experience when confronted with various forms of peer pressure.

Talk about it. Discuss which peer pressure situations would be or have been most stressful, and which forms of peer pressure would be the hardest to resist, and why.

Reproducible Worksheet 11.3

Think it Out!, asks students to practice the skill of "stopping and thinking" about the consequences of acting on various impulses associated with peer pressure. Ask students to list some impulses and consequences that may occur with each scenario.

Talk about it. Discuss which impulses would be appropriate/inappropriate to act on.

Reproducible Worksheet 11.4

"No" isn't a Bad Word, asks students to practice ways of withstanding peer pressure. Ask students to fill in circles surrounding the scenario with various ways of saying "no."

Talk about it. Discuss some of the ways students chose to say "no" to the peer pressure depicted in the scenario. Discuss not always having to "be nice" when responding to peer pressure.

Reproducible Worksheet 11.5

Examining My Resistance to Peer Pressure, asks students to think of two (2) times when they have resisted peer pressure and to identify their successful thoughts and behaviors

Talk about it. Ask students if they would like to share either of their experiences resisting peer pressure. Discuss how thinking is a strength in resisting peer pressure.

Peer Pressure Crossword

Complete the Peer Pressure Crossword using the words at the bottom of the page.

ACROSS

2. Friends may pressure you to wear a certain brand of ___________.
4. ____ is helpful word to withstand peer pressure.
5. ________ control can help you to withstand peer pressure.
7. Someone may offer you ________ and say "Everyone is doing it."
8. Some of your closest ________ may even pressure you.

DOWN

1. People may tease or _______ you to get you to do something.
2. A classmate may ask you to help them ________ on a test.
3. The pressure to be _________ at school may be a form of peer pressure.
5. A friend may _______ you to a party where there are drugs or alcohol.
6. A ______ is a behavior that is widely accepted.

popular, friends, taunt, norm, no, impulse, alcohol, invite, clothes, cheat

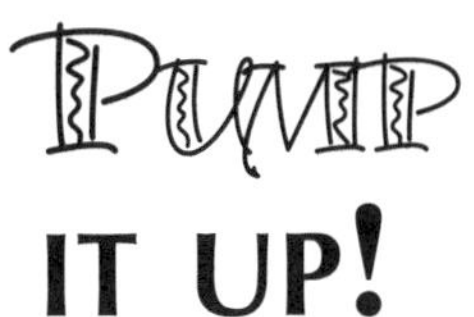

IT UP!

Listed below are examples of situations where kids feel peer pressure. Rate the amount of weight or pressure you might feel with a similar situation.

1. **Your friend is doing poorly in English. S/he says it would really help his/her grade if you let him/her copy your homework assignment.**

   5 lbs. 25 lbs. 100 lbs. 1000 lbs.

2. **You are hanging out with some people after school and a couple of them are smoking. They pass you the pack of cigarettes.**

   5 lbs. 25 lbs. 100 lbs. 1000 lbs.

3. **You've been hanging out with a new group of kids at school and they all wear the same brands of clothes. You can't afford some of the brands that they wear.**

   5 lbs. 25 lbs. 100 lbs. 1000 lbs.

4. **You are hanging out with some of your friends during lunch. They are all making fun of another student whom is sitting near by. Everyone in the group has said something negative about the other student and now they are all looking over at you.**

   5 lbs. 25 lbs. 100 lbs. 1000 lbs.

5. **Your friend has taken another friend's scooter without permission and asks if you want to go for a ride.**

   5 lbs. 25 lbs. 100 lbs. 1000 lbs.

6. **All of your friends have signed-up for the soccer team and want you to sign-up too, but you really don't want to play.**

   5 lbs. 25 lbs. 100 lbs. 1000 lbs.

IT OUT!

Read the following scenarios. Write an impulse and a consequence for acting on that impulse for each scenario.

1. **Your mom asked you to come directly home after school and help pick up the house before your little brothers birthday party. On the way home one of your friends tells you that s/he just got a new video game and asks if you want to come over and play it.**

IMPULSE	CONSEQUENCE

2. **You are walking through the mall and see a shirt that you really want, but you don't have enough money to pay for the shirt.**

IMPULSE	CONSEQUENCE

"NO" Isn't a Bad Word

It's ok to say "no" when someone is pressuring you to do something wrong. Practice withstanding peer pressure by brainstorming various ways to say "No" to the given situation and writing them in the circles.

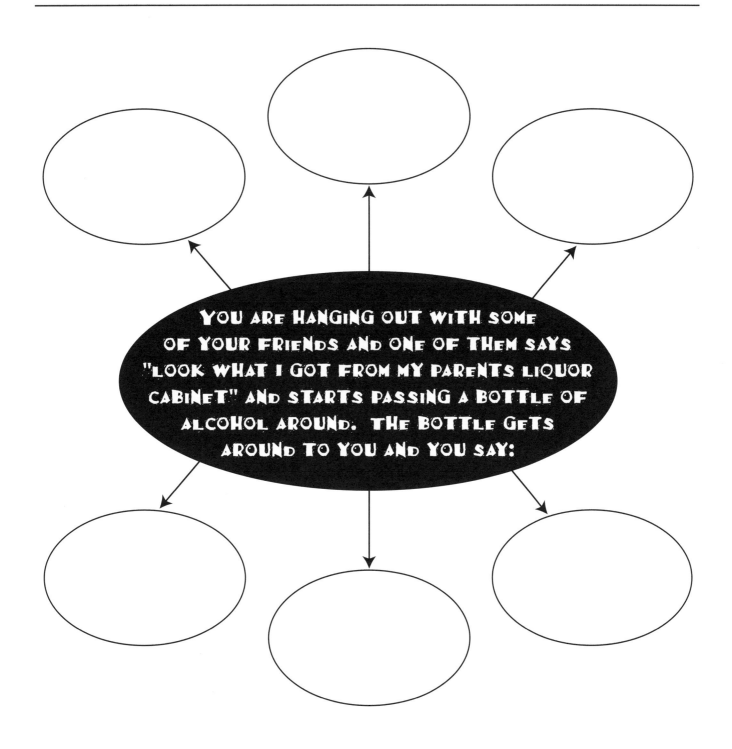

YOU ARE HANGING OUT WITH SOME OF YOUR FRIENDS AND ONE OF THEM SAYS "LOOK WHAT I GOT FROM MY PARENTS LIQUOR CABINET" AND STARTS PASSING A BOTTLE OF ALCOHOL AROUND. THE BOTTLE GETS AROUND TO YOU AND YOU SAY:

Examining My Resistance to Peer Pressure

Think of some times when you felt compelled to give in to peer pressure but didn't. Analyze these by completing the following rubric.

	TEMPTATION	*WHAT DID YOU TELL YOURSELF?*	*WHAT DID YOU DO?*
(1)			
(2)			
(3)			

Boyfriends and Girlfriends: Is it Love or is it Drama and Chaos?

Lesson 12

Objective:

At the end of this lesson students will be able to

- Describe how to identify if someone is truly attracted or not
- Distinguish the differences between love and control
- Recognize the traits of a healthy affectionate relationship
- Identify ways to stop gossip and "drama"

Materials Needed:

Pens/pencils, paper, a copy of Appendix F, tape, scissors, a large ball, ten (10) copies of Appendix G, construction paper, and scissors

Script:

I think that all of us would agree that it is a wonderful feeling to have a girlfriend or boyfriend. To feel loved is a basic human need and all of us look for it in one way or another. Sometimes, though, we may rush into these romantic relationships without thinking and then experience all kinds of problems. It's always good to stop and think if this is a person or a relationship that is good for us.

Once involved in romantic relationships we may feel overly jealous or controlling, or we may miscommunicate, or we may not know how to balance someone else's needs with our own. We may expect ideal love instead of realistic love. None of this makes for a healthy relationship. We will be covering a lot of ground in this unit regarding good decision making in girl/boyfriend relationships.

Rationale:

Romantic relationships are important contributors to teens' identity and social development (Connolly and Goldberg, 1999; Erikson, 1968). Since middle school is often the time when romantic relationships begin, it is essential that we teach teens how to stop and think about these important relationships.

Impulsive teens often have similar problems in romantic relationships that they have in their other peer relationships (i.e. intrusiveness, not listening, not cooperating, emotional melt-downs, etc.). In addition to these problems, impulsive teens can also be obsessive about romantic interests and very sensation-seeking in the relationship.

Discussion Questions:

- Have you ever gossiped about other people's love lives? What was the outcome of this? What is the difference between gossip and sharing information?
- Have you ever found yourself in a romantic relationship that you didn't want to be in because you impulsively said "yes" to someone? Why would it be good to stop and think about who you go with?
- If you really like someone as a girl/boyfriend, how many times a week should you call them? How many times is too many times? What might happen if you called too much?
- How do you decide how physical to get with a girlfriend or boyfriend?

Activities:

Have students divide up into small groups of 3-4 students. Give each group a pen/pencil and a piece of paper and ask them to create a "list of rules" for healthy romantic relationships (i.e. "Couples should listen to each other without interrupting," "Couples should trust each other," etc.).

Explain to the students that potential girl/boyfriends may ask them to do things that they are unsure about. Often times it is a good idea to take some time to think about these things (i.e. Do you want to be my girl/boyfriend? Do you want hang out Friday night? etc.). Have students divide up into small groups of 3-4 students and make a list of possible questions that they might face. Then direct them to write down different ways in which they can politely say, "I need more time to think about it."

Ask different pairs of students to role-play scenarios where one of them tries to gossip about a couple of other peers' romantic intentions (i.e. breaking up, getting together, etc.) and the other one either (a) politely says that s/he is not interested in listening or (b) distracts the speaker away from that topic.

Explain to students that when two (2) people have going out for awhile and then decide to separate, it can be very painful and awkward. Often times this is when very unkind things are said. Using the statements in Appendix F, cut these out and tape each one onto a different spot on a basketball or volleyball (or any ball of comparable size). Ask students to stand in a circle. Then direct them to slowly toss the ball to one another (making sure that everyone gets included). Each time that a student catches the ball, s/he is to read the statement that is facing her/him as a response to breaking up with someone.

Cut out ten (10) "stepping stones" from construction paper (a template is provided in Appendix G) and number them 1 – 10. On the opposite side of each "stepping stone," write one of the following scenarios (one scenario for each "stepping stone"):

- Sara told Abby that she heard that Antoine and Tameca had broken up.
- Dakota told Parker that he thought Semah was cute.
- Jeremy told Rachel that he thought she was the prettiest girl in the school.
- Jessica told Thomas that Chan told Lian that Josh had cheated on Elizabeth.
- Tyrell told Trameca that he didn't want a girlfriend right now.
- William told Conner that he overheard Sean say that Madeline snuck out of the house to meet Aiden.
- Brittany told Megan that she thought Kyle liked her.
- Abby told Michael that she thought Jerome was flirting with his girlfriend.
- Carlos told Phillip that he had heard rumors about what a bad reputation Brianne had.
- Tiffany told Kim that she had heard that Kim's boyfriend had made the winning goal in the last school soccer game.

Then place the "stepping stones" scenario-side down (numbered side up) in a circle. Play some music while students walk in a circle on the "stepping stones." At different time intervals, make the music stop. Instruct students to stop moving when the music stops and to stand on the "stepping stone" that they have stepped on when the music stopped. Ask the student standing on "stepping stone" #1 to turn it over, read it aloud and then to state whether the situation is gossiping or sharing information. Continue playing and stopping the music until all of the "stepping stones" have been read.

How To Use Reproducible Sheets:

Reproducible Worksheet 12.1

Loves Me, Loves Me Not, uses the petals of a daisy in the classic "He loves me; he loves me not" verse to have students write down the behaviors of one who may or may not be interested in them as girl/boyfriend. Examples such as "finds reasons to hang out with me" and "doesn't return my phone calls" are given.

Talk about it. Ask students why it would be important to be able to read the signs of whether or not someone had feelings for them. Discuss what might happen if they thought someone had feelings and s/he really didn't; then ask what might happen if they thought someone did not have feelings and s/he really did.

Reproducible Worksheet 12.2

What is Real Love? allows students to compare the notions of idealized love with rational, real life love. They are asked to write down characteristics of romanticized love and contrast these concepts with realistic love.

Talk about it. Ask students to discuss why romanticized love can be damaging to a relationship. Discuss how expectations affect feelings and behaviors.

Reproducible Worksheet 12.3

Gossip or Sharing Information? asks students to consider the difference between gossip and sharing information. It then asks them to write down five (5) distinguishing characteristics that help one to decide if something is gossip or sharing information.

Talk about it. Ask students to share their "rules" for knowing the difference between gossip and sharing information. Discuss how gossip is damaging and why people might want to gossip. If appropriate, ask students if they would like to share any personal experiences being the victim of gossip.

Reproducible Worksheet 12.4

Don't Control or Be Controlled, uses a 'Yes/No' format to ask students to consider their girl/boyfriend's controlling behavior as well as their own. The end of the sheet suggests that a 'Yes' answer to any of the questions is cause for consideration regarding the health of the relationship.

Talk about it. Explain to students that sometimes people confuse control for love. Ask them to describe how they understand the two things to be different.

Reproducible Worksheet 12.5

Making Those Difficult Decisions, asks students to read over typical adolescent dilemmas involving boyfriends and girlfriends. It then asks them to select one of three responses to each dilemma.

Talk about it. Ask students if they have ever encountered any of the situations that were described. Ask them how they handled it and then, if they had it to do over again, how they would handle it and why.

Loves Me; Loves Me Not

Stop and think about the signs that might tell whether or not someone likes you as a girl/boyfriend. On the white petals of the daisy below, write in some of the signs that show someone likes you (for example, "finds reasons to hang out with me"); on the gray petals, write in some of the signs that show someone might not like you (for example, "doesn't return my phone calls").

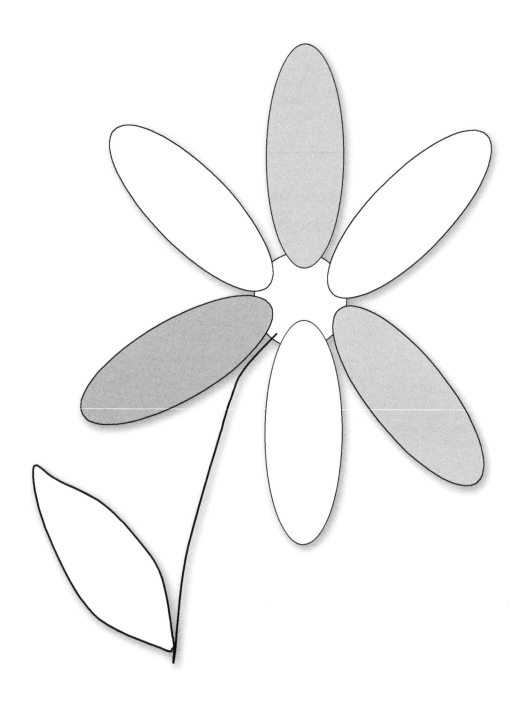

WHAT IS REAL LOVE?

Some people view love through rose-colored glasses. They think that love should always be perfect (even though the people involved are imperfect!). Consider some of your romanticized (unrealistic) ideas of love. Write them in the left column and then write a more realistic view of love on the right column. An example is given for you.

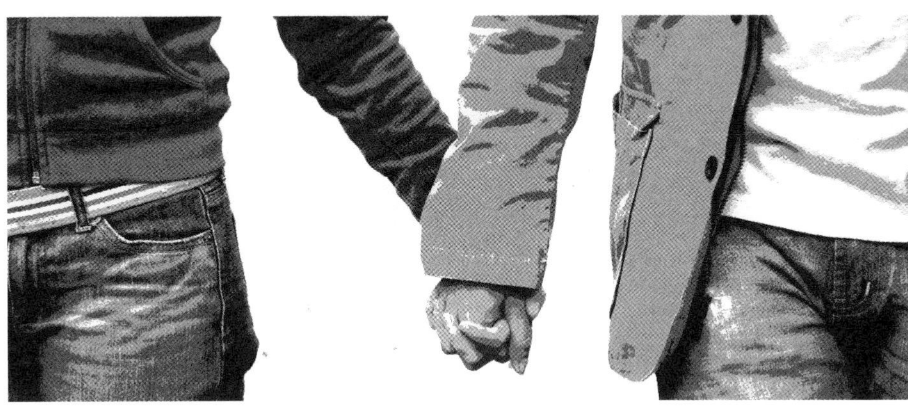

Romanticized (Unrealistic) View of Love	*Realistic View of Love*
Couples who love each other should make each other happy 100% of the time.	Couples can still care for one another when they don't agree - and can get on each other's nerves when they spend too much time together.

Gossip or Sharing Information?

It's fun to talk with friends about things that are interesting. However, sometimes this can turn into gossip which leads to "drama" and hurt feelings. What do you think is the difference between gossiping and sharing information? Write down five (5) "rules" that distinguish the two.

1.

2.

3.

4.

5.

Don't Control or Be Controlled

Read the following questions and answer honestly.

1. Do you or your girl/boyfriend get offended when the other one spends time with her/his other friends?

   YES **NO**

2. Do you or your girl/boyfriend ever check each other's wallets, purses, phone calls or text messages?

   YES **NO**

3. Do you or your girl/boyfriend get upset if you can't see each other every day?

   YES **NO**

4. Do you or your girl/boyfriend get easily jealous or accuse each other of cheating?

   YES **NO**

5. Do you or your girl/boyfriend ever change your plans because the other one told you to?

   YES **NO**

6. Do you or your girl/boyfriend ever tell each other what to wear?

   YES **NO**

7. Do you or your girl/boyfriend feel like you have to drop everything when the other wants something?

   YES **NO**

If you answered 'YES' to any of these questions, you may need to think about how healthy your relationship really is. Healthy relationships consist of individuals who let the other person have freedom and don't try to control one another.

Making Those Difficult Decisions

Read the following situations and the three (3) possible responses. Stop and think about the best way to handle the situation and circle the letter that corresponds to the correct answer. Discuss with your class or group.

1. **You are talking with a classmate of the opposite sex from history class, and your girlfriend/boyfriend walks by. S/he completely loses her/his temper and accuses you of cheating.**
   a) Scream back at her/him that you are not doing anything wrong
   b) Slap her/him for being so rude
   c) Say, "Excuse me" to your classmate and then privately tell your boyfriend/girlfriend that her/his behavior is embarrassing and that you have the right to have friends of the opposite sex

2. **Your girlfriend/boyfriend told you that s/he had to go to dinner with her/his parents that night but later you saw her/him with someone else at the movies and the two of them were holding hands.**
   a) Pretend like nothing happened
   b) Call your girlfriend/boyfriend and explain that you saw her/him at the movies and that you can not let yourself be with someone that you cannot trust
   c) Tell all your friends what a creep your girlfriend/boyfriend is

3. **You just found out that your parents are getting divorced and you are very upset. Your girlfriend/boyfriend asks you what is wrong.**
   a) Pretend everything is OK and say, "Nothing's wrong"
   b) Explain about your parents and tell your girlfriend/boyfriend that it will be nice to have her/his support during this difficult time
   c) Lie and say that you are not feeling well

4. **Your girlfriend/boyfriend is pressuring you to go "farther" and do more physically with her/him than you are comfortable with.**
   a) Say nothing and go ahead and do it
   b) Complain but go ahead and do it
   c) Tell her/him that you are not comfortable and that you hope your relationship is more than just physical attraction

5. **It seems that whenever you and your girlfriend/boyfriend hang out with friends, that it is always with her/his friends and not with yours. Your friends are starting to complain that they never see you any more.**
   a) Tell your girlfriend/boyfriend that you would like for the two of you to take turns spending time with your friends and with her/his friends
   b) Tell your friends that that your girlfriend/boyfriend is more important to you
   c) Tell your friends that they are just being silly

REFERENCES

Asher, S.R., & Coie, J.D. (eds). (1990). Peer rejection in childhood. New York: Cambridge University Press.

Bembenutty, H., Karabenick, S.A. (1998). Academic delay of gratification. Learning and Individual Differences, 10(4), 329-346.

Ciarrochi, J., Chan, A., & Baigar, J. (2001). Measuring emotional intelligence in adolescents. Personality and Individual Differences, 31(7), 1105-1119.

Cicchetti, D. & Howes, P.W. (1991). Developmental psychopathology in the context of the family: Illustrations from the study of child maltreatment. Canadian Journal of Behavioral Science, 23, 257-281.

Corapci, F. (2008). The role of child temperament on head start preschoolers' social competence in the context of cumulative risk. Journal of Applied Developmental Psychology, 29(1).

d'Acremont, M. & Van der Lindon, M. (2007). How is impulsivity related to depression in adolescence? Evidence from a French validation of the cognitive emotion regulation questionnaire. Journal of Adolescence, 30(2), 271-282.

Dougherty, D.M., Dew, R.E., Mathias, C.W., Marsh, D.M., Addicott, M.A., & Barratt, E.S. (2007). Impulsive and premeditated subtypes of aggression in conduct disorder: Differences in time estimation. Aggressive Behavior, 33 (6), 574-582.

Fischhoff, B. (1992). Risk taking: A developmental perspective. In J.F. Yates (Ed.), Risk-Taking Behavior, (pp. 133-162). Chichester, England: John Wiley & Sons.

Ganzel, A.K. (1999). Adolescent decision making: The influence of mood, age, and gender on the consideration of information [Electronic version]. Journal of Adolescent Research, 14, 289-318.

Gardner, M. & Steinberg, L. (2005). Peer Influence on Risk Taking, Risk Preference, and Risky Decision Making in Adolescents and Adulthood: An Experimental Study. Developmental Psychology, 41(4), 625-635.

Hanna, F.J. & Hunt, W.P. (1999). Techniques for psychotherapy with defiant, aggressive adolescents. Psychotherapy: Theory, Research, Practice, Training, 36(1), 56-68.

Harris, K. R., Fridlander, B.D., Saddler, B., Frizzelle, R. & Graham, S. (2005). Self-Monitoring of Attention Versus Self-Monitoring of Academic Performance: Effects Among Students with ADHD in the General Education Classroom. The Journal of Special Education, 39(3), 145-156.

Kerig, P.K. (2005). Revisiting the construct of boundary dissolution: A multidimensional perspective. Journal of Emotional Abuse, 5(2/3), 5-42.

Kochanska, G., & Aksan, N. (2006). Children's conscience and self-regulation. Journal of Personality, 74(6), 1587-1617.

References

Landau, S. & Moore, L.A. (1991). Social skill deficits in children with attention deficit hyperactivity disorder. School Psychology Review, 20, 235-251.

Mack, D., Strong, H. & Kowalski, Kent, C. (2007). Does friendship matter? An examination of social physique anxiety in adolescence. Journal of Applied Social Psychology, 37(6), 1248-1264.

Miranda, A., Jarque, S. & Tarraga, R. (2006). Interventions in School Settings for Students With ADHD. Exceptionality, 14(1), 35-52.

Morrongiello, B & Dawber, T. (2004). Identifying Factors that Relate to Children's Risk-Taking Decisions. Canadian Journal of Behavioural Science, 36(4), 255-266.

Mott, P. & Krane A. (1994). Interpersonal cognitive problem-solving and childhood social competence. Cognitive Therapy and Research,18(2), 127-141.

Mulsow, M., O'Neal, K., & Murry, V. (2001). Adult attention-deficit disorder, the family and child maltreatment. Trauma, Violence, & Abuse, 2(1), 36-41.

McMahon, S. D.; Washburn, J. J. (2003). Violence prevention : An evaluation of program effects with urban African American students. Journal of Primary Prevention, 24(1), 43-62.

McMurran, M., Blair, M., and Egan, V. (2002). An investigation of the correlations between aggression, impulsiveness, social problem-solving, and alcohol use. Aggressive Behavior, 28, 439-334.

Olson, S. L. (1989). Assessment of Impulsivity in preschoolers: Cross measure convergences, longitudinal stability and relevance to social competence. Journal of Clinical Child Psychology, 18(2), 176-183.

Patterson, C.M., & Newman, J.P. (1993). Reflectivity and learning from aversive events: Toward a psychological mechanism for the syndromes of disinhibition. Psychological Review, 100 (4) 716-736.

Silk, J. S., Vanderbilt-Adriance, E., Shaw, D. S., Forbes, E. E., Whalen, D. J., Ryan, N. D., & Dahl, R. e. (2007). Resilience among children and adolescents at risk for depression: Mediation and moderation across social and neurobiological context. Development and Psychopathology, 19(3), 841-865.

Silk, J. S., Steinberg, L., & Morris, A. S. (2003). Adolescents' Emotion Regulation in Daily life: Links to depression symptoms and problem behavior. Child Development, 74(6), 1869-1880.

Susman, E.J., Inoff-Germain, G., Nottlemann, E.D., Loriaux, D.L., Cutler, G.B. Jr. & Ghrousos, G.P. (1987). Hormones, Emotional, Dispositions, and Aggressive Attributes in Young Adolescents. Child Development, 58(4), 1114-1134.

REFERENCES

Weinberger, D.A. (1997). Distress and Self-Restraint as Measures of Adjustment Across the Life Span: Confirmatory Factor Analyses in clinical and Nonclinical Samples. Psychological Assessment, 9(2), 132-135.

White, J.L., Moffitt, T.E., Caspi, A., Bartusch, D. J., Needles, D. J., & Stouthamer-Loeber, M. (1994). Measuring impulsivity and examining its relationship to delinquency. Journal of Abnormal Psychology, 103(2), 192-205.

Appendix

Pros and Cons

Karen spent the night with a friend. While she was at the friend's house, the parents went out to a movie for a couple of hours. Karen's parents have forbidden her to be at friends' houses unless the parents are home. Karen thought about the following solutions: (1) Not say anything and just stay at the friend's house, (2) Call her parents to come get her, (3) take advantage of the situation and invite some boys over. She decides on #1. What are the pros and cons of making this choice?

Jamal finally made the football team after two years of trying. However, his performance is not as good as he would like it to be. He thought about several solutions including (1) Taking steroids to improve his strength, (2) Working out more, (3) Getting advice from his coach regarding what he could do to improve. He decides on # 2. What are the pros and cons of making this choice?

Jeremy is new this year to his school and wants to make some friends. He discussed it with his grandmother and came up with these ideas:
(1) Join some clubs, (2) Hang around after school and start up some conversations with kids, (3) Start inviting kids over to his house. He decides that he would like to try #2. What are the pros and cons of making this choice?

Jackie has gained some weight over the last few months and kids are starting to tease her about it. She would really like to lose a few pounds and considers the following options: (1) Walk three miles before school every morning, (2) Join a gym, (3) Buy some diet pills from drug store. She decides that she would like to try #1. What are the pros and cons of making this choice?

Kim accidentally found out from a cousin that she is adopted. This came as quite a shock to her and she would like to talk to her mother about it but doesn't know how to bring it up. She considered the following: (1) Ask her mother to take her to lunch and bring it up then, (2) Ask her cousin to tell her mother what happened so that her mother would approach her, (3) Ask her about it some Sunday afternoon when she is not busy. She decides that she would like to try #3. What are the pros and cons of making this choice?

Kevin's parents argue every night. It often gets so loud that Kevin cannot even think. His grades are starting to fall because of it. Kevin thinks about: (1) Telling his parents how their fighting affects him, (2) Running away from home, (3) Turning his music up really, really loud so he cannot hear them. He decides that he would like to try #1. What are the pros and cons of making this choice?

Pros and Cons

Angelica wants to let Alberto know that she likes him more than as a friend, but she is not sure how he feels about her. She thought about the following solutions: (1) Write him a note and pass it to him in class, (2) Tell him directly on the telephone some evening, (3) Have a friend tell him. She decides that she would like to try #3. What are the pros and cons of making this choice?

Daniel just went to live with his grandmother after being in foster care for a year. His grandmother is very religious and takes him to church with her three times a week. Daniel loves living with his grandmother, but hates going to church so much. He has considered (1) Refusing to go with her anymore, (2) Asking her if he could just go one time a week, (3) Talking to his case worker about the problem. He decides that he would like to try #2. What are the pros and cons of making this choice?

Claudia and her friend want to go to the movies together but don't agree on which one to see. They think about (1) Flipping a coin, (2) Going to see both movies, (3) Choosing a 3rd movie. They decide that they would like to try #3. What are the pros and cons of making this choice?

Peyton has always had a good complexion but lately he has broken out with a really bad case of acne. He would definitely like to get rid of it but doesn't know how. His mother suggests (1) See a dermatologist, (2) Buy some acne medicine at the drug store, (3) Wash his face more often. He decides that he would like to try #1. What are the pros and cons of making this choice?

Connor just found out that his best friend, Peter, has been using drugs. Connor is very upset and wants to do something but is not sure what would be the right thing. He thinks about: (1) Confronting his friend, (2) Telling his friend's parents, (3) Ignoring it. He decides that he would like to try #2. What are the pros and cons of making this choice?

Carmetta lost a very important assignment the day before it was due. She looked everywhere and now thinks that it may have accidentally gotten thrown away. She considers the following solutions: (1) Stay up all night and do it over, (2) Take an 'F,' (3) Call her teacher at home and ask for an extension. She decides that she would like to try #1. What are the pros and cons of making this choice?

Cognitive Distortions

All-or-nothing thinking - Thinking of things in absolute terms, like "always," "every," or "never."

Jumping to conclusions - Assuming something negative where there is no evidence to support it (i.e. assuming the intents of others).

Magnification - Exaggerating the way people or situations truly are. Another name for this is catastrophizing.

Personalization - Assuming you or others directly caused things when that may not have been the case.

Perfectionistic thinking - Thinking that things have to be a certain exact way in order to be okay. It uses words like "should," "ought," and "have to."

Disqualifying the positive - Continually negating or "shooting down" positive experiences.

Overgeneralization - Taking isolated cases and using them to make wide generalizations.

Mental filter - Focusing exclusively on certain, small negative aspects of something while ignoring the greater positive aspects.

Anxiety Situation Cards

It is you first day at a new school and you don't know anyone.	*You lost one of your dad's tools.*
You are planning on telling your parents about a bad grade.	*You have to give a speech in front of a group of people.*
You are going to ask a girl/guy you like to go out with you.	*You are walking through a scary place at night.*
You are about to take a long math test.	*You trip and fall down in front of a large crowd of kids and they are laughing.*
A bully at school is calling you names.	*You are attempting to jump off the high dive at the public swimming pool.*

Anger Situation Cards

While sitting in class someone from behind you throws a piece of paper which hits you in the back of the head.	*Another student calls a member of your family a bad name.*
You have spent a lot of time playing a video game and have made it to the final stage. Your younger sibling walks by and accidentally unplugs the game console requiring you to start over.	*Your parents have promised to take you and a friend somewhere special this weekend but when your friend arrives, your parents tell you they changed their mind, and it will have to be some other time.*
Someone takes something that belongs to you and refuses to give it back.	*You are playing kickball and one player on your team keeps striking out. Your team only needs one more run to win, the bases are loaded and the player who keeps striking out is up to kick. The player strikes out again and your team loses the game.*
You are grounded and will not be able to hang out with your friends for an entire week.	*Someone you know is spreading rumors about you having a crush on someone that you absolutely do not have a crush on!*
Your teacher accuses you of talking when you were only trying to better understand the assignment.	*Your teacher gives you detention for simply rolling your eyes at her.*

Peer Pressure Situation Cards

"Hey, I have the answers to Mrs. Hansen's test. Hurry up and copy them down."

"Your jeans are totally out of style, if you want to hang out with us you better go shopping."

"Dude, just try it, cigarettes really calm me down."

"It's just one beer. Don't be scared, everyone drinks now a days."

"I don't really feel like staying at school today, let's leave at lunch and play video games at my house."

"Come on, every one is doing it. If you don't have a girl/boy-friend, everyone will think you are weird."

"Don't be chicken. Just take it; no one will know and I already dared you to do it."

"Hey, the party will be going all night and all the cool people will be there. Just tell your mom that you are staying the night at my house and I will tell my parents that I'm staying at your house."

Break-up Situation Cards

"S/he is a good person. We just weren't right for each other."	*"I know that we will be able to be friends after we get over our hurts."*
"No one is going to trick me into talking bad about __________."	*"Even though we are not together, I still wish the best for ____________."*
"It's better to have loved and lost than to never have loved at all."	*"I know that both of us are good people and will handle ourselves appropriately now that we are not together."*
"Breaking up is hard but it's not going to get the best of me."	*"Just because we broke up does not mean we have to hate each other."*

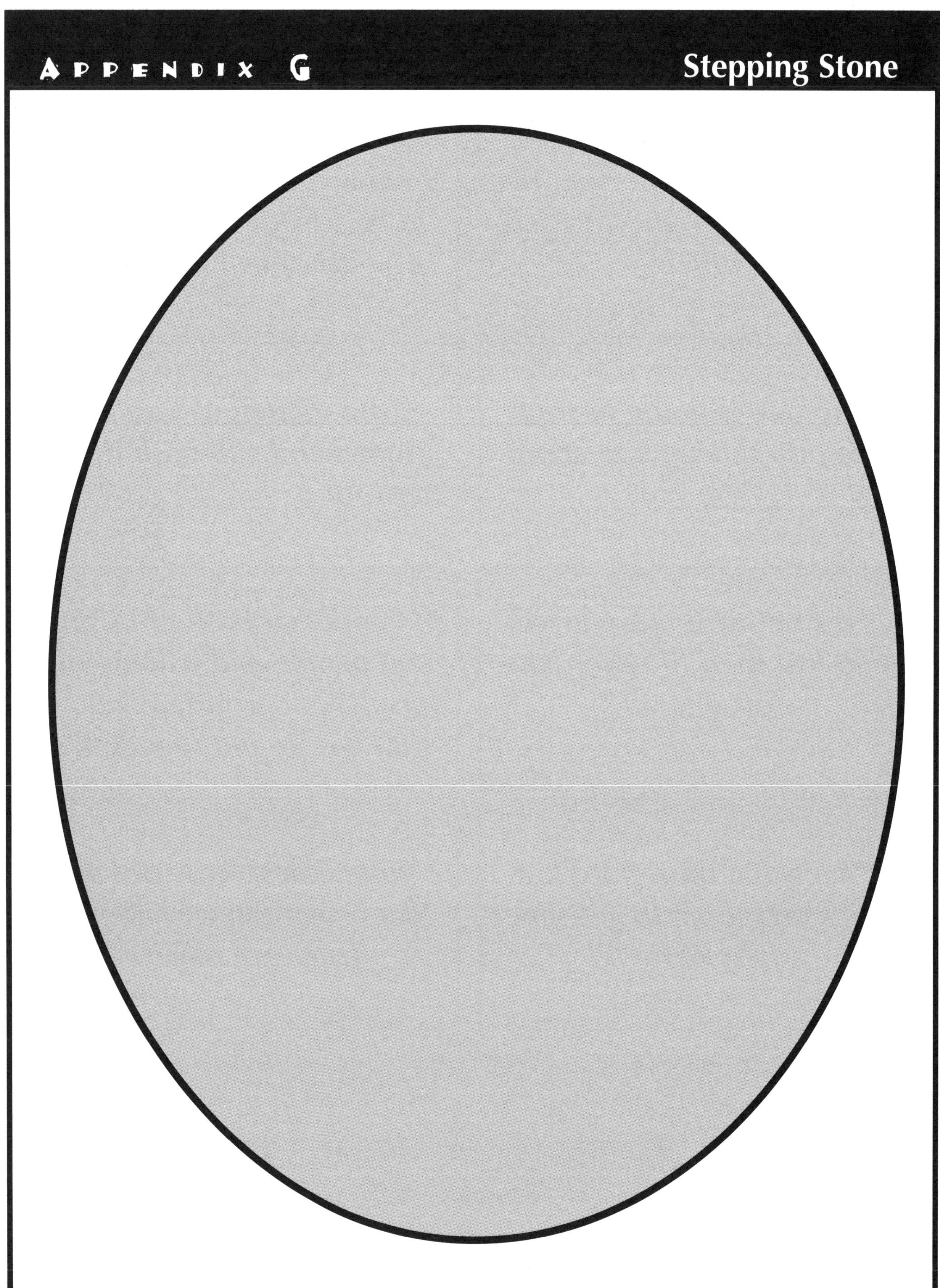